THE MAGICAL TEACHERS OF HARRY POTTER

HOGWARTS TEACHING STYLES UNRAVELED

DANIELLE DICKIE

Teachistry

Published in the United States by:
Teachistry
www.teachistry.com

ISBN: 978-0-578-70402-9

Note: Some names have been altered to protect those known to the author.

Editor: Jason Dickie
Front cover art: Chris Howard SaltwaterWitch.com

The author is not affiliated with J.K. Rowling, Scholastic or Bloomsbury. This book is an independent and unauthorized fan publication. It is a literary analysis of the Harry Potter series and does not imply any recommendation or affiliation with the Harry Potter franchise. It is meant to further scholarship and is not a spin-off, companion volume, sequel or prequel to the Harry Potter series.

All references to the Harry Potter novels are taken from the following American editions, published by Scholastic, Inc., in New York: *Sorcerer's Stone* (1998); *Chamber of Secrets* (1999); *Prisoner of Azkaban* (1999); *Goblet of Fire* (2000); *Order of the Phoenix* (2003); *Half-Blood Prince* (2005); *Deathly Hallows* (2007).

CONTENTS

INTRODUCTION

"And do you learn much, up at the school?"
"Erm — A bit," said Hermione timidly.
"A bit. Well, that's something."[1]

I have made the journey to Hogwarts more times than Harry. Sure, my means of transportation aren't as impressive as his, but the experience is just as magical. I grew up alongside Harry, Ron and Hermione, and I could always count on Hogwarts to welcome me home. As I entered the teaching world, my love for Harry Potter persisted. My first year in the classroom was horrible with too many late nights, little adult interaction and more crying than I like to admit. The stress of that first year was too much to handle and I was desperate for an escape. So I returned, once again, to the wizarding world. As I read the books and watched the movies, I was finally able to forget my troubles.

But something just as magical happened, I made connections between my teaching experiences and the professors at Hogwarts. While I was trying to determine what type of teacher I wanted to become, I realized I was learning from these familiar pages in a new way. Was I a strict authoritarian like Professor Snape? Or a push-over like Hagrid? Would I be able to reach the Nevilles of the world like Professor Sprout? Or would I be plagued with feelings of inadequacy like Professor Trelawney? It's amazing what these seven wonderful books and eight movies can teach us about the effectiveness of different teaching styles. I began to question J.K. Rowling's true calling. Was she an accomplished writer or an education expert?

Prior to becoming a published writer, J.K. Rowling was a teacher so it makes sense that her professors would feel real. She does such a tremendous job at writing well-rounded, multidimensional characters that it is easy to picture them in the classroom setting. Other than their wands and strange attire, some of the Hogwarts professors would fit right alongside myself and my colleagues at our school site.

As both a student and a teacher myself, I have witnessed teachers who motivated and believed in students as well as Professor McGonagall. I have had teachers who would spend an entire period talking about themselves like Professor Lockhart or droning on like Binns. And we might think there's no way a teacher can be a vindictive bully like Snape, but ask any student and I'm sure they can name a teacher who has bullied one of their peers, whether intentionally or not.

Before we get to Harry Potter's professors, I need to begin with this disclaimer: I am not really a magical teacher. The only wand I have is the one I bought at Universal Studios. Sure, it allows me to open locks, play music and shoot water out of a fountain inside the theme park, but outside those gates it does nothing to cover up the mistakes I make on a daily basis. If I was attending Hogwarts I would be one of the unnamed characters in the background and I know for certain I would never be invited to join the Slug Club. I'm just an ordinary Muggle teacher, trying to make the most out of myself and my students. I'm not even close to being the best teacher at my school site. So what makes me qualified to write a book about teaching? These negative thoughts made me want to quit writing more times than Neville forgot the password to Gryffindor's common room. But after closely examining the Hogwarts professors, I came to the realization that no teacher is perfect. Teaching is a constant work in progress and every one of us is learning and adapting until the very end.

In my experience, however, teaching books seem to suggest the opposite. The education section in any bookstore is filled with stories of success, charity and perfection. These books focus on teachers who give everything, including their left kidney, to their students. These idealized teachers have transfigured the worst children into Harvard law professors, movies are written about them and they travel to the White House to win lavish awards. I don't want to take anything away from their accomplishments, but these aren't the teachers we see in our schools. Great teaching isn't always defined by this level of success. Most great teachers get overlooked and forgotten by all but their students.

These books fail to capture the true nature of teaching—it's messy. Young students often believe their teachers are infallible and this myth carries over to our adult lives. As well as actually teaching our subjects, we are expected to be counselors, mentors, disciplinarians and coaches simultaneously. This is a lot to handle. Anyone working in a school system knows that not every child is successful, not every lesson is perfect and not every teacher is great. But all great teachers have a desire to grow in order to better serve the needs of their students.

This is where analyzing fictional teachers gives a distinct advantage. Have you ever seen an education book about a teacher who abuses their students? Well, flip straight to Professor Umbridge's chapter and read about the effect this can have. But that is a bit extreme. Of course there aren't education books written about these teachers—it would be horrific. What about a teacher who feels they're worthless? Or one that plays favorites? Or a teacher who is so nervous that their students aren't learning? These types of teachers aren't being written about because they're not what society views as spectacular. Yet this might have described you. I certainly have some of these characteristics, but I also know my teaching style isn't fully defined by these issues. What better way to grow as an educator than to learn from these familiar professors' strengths and weaknesses?

Each chapter of this book focuses on one Hogwarts professor. I will describe their interactions with their students and compare them with my own experiences in the classroom, both good and bad. Just as the Hogwarts professors aren't flawless, the stories I share aren't from the position of an expert, but from an imperfect teacher striving to be better. I have taught history in both a middle school and a high school in California's Central Valley. The landscape and subject matter may be different from that of Hogwarts, but the students I teach are just as diverse, difficult and wonderful. I have learned there is no one-size-fits-all solution when it comes to working with students and the same holds true for teachers. Every teacher and classroom are unique, Hogwarts included.

I have grouped each of the professors into five sections: Heads of Houses, Electives and Their Emergency Replacements, Core Classes, Defense Against the Dark Arts, and Harry and the Headmaster. The chapters are meant to be read in order, as I will compare the professors within each section, but feel free to skip around. If you're tired of reading about boring Professor Binns then skip a few chapters to Professor Lupin. By all means, read the chapters backwards starting with Professor Dumbledore. I'm sure he would approve of this quirkiness.

As you read, I hope you are able to pull ideas from all the Hogwarts professors to implement into your teaching style as I have, ensuring you engage your students, walk alongside them as they discover their individuality and help them contribute to society. Even if you don't have the official title, everyone is a teacher in some capacity. Parents teach their children about the world, managers teach their employees new skills, and when we fearlessly pursue our dreams in the face of adversity we teach those around us to do the same. Even if this doesn't describe you, any

Harry Potter fan can appreciate reading more about the Hogwarts teachers who have already taught us so much. Harry's professors show us there isn't just one spell you can cast to become a perfect teacher—every day Muggle teachers of all kinds bring true magic into their classrooms.

PART I: HEADS OF HOUSES

PROFESSOR SPROUT

*

PROFESSOR FLITWICK

*

PROFESSOR MCGONAGALL

*

PROFESSOR SNAPE

*

PROFESSOR SLUGHORN

PROFESSOR SPROUT

ACCEPTING * COLLABORATIVE

"I feel that if a single pupil wants to come, then the school ought to remain open for that pupil."[1]

HEAD OF HUFFLEPUFF * HERBOLOGY

As Head of Hufflepuff House, Pomona Sprout is a dedicated, hard-working and kind woman. She is described as a squat, dumpy little witch and is often seen covered in dirt. Harry takes Herbology all six years he attends Hogwarts, and yet Professor Sprout exists mostly in the periphery. Scenes in her classroom tend to focus on students battling magical plants rather than any straightforward instructional material, and she is rarely seen when tensions in the story rise. Since we barely get the chance to see her speaking to the class, I struggled to figure out just what type of teaching style she employs. Of the Heads of Houses, I prefer to tell people I am like Professor McGonagall, but in reality I'm more like Professor Sprout. I exist in the background. After teaching history for several years, I still had coworkers asking if I was the new science teacher. I'm more recognizable among the students than the staff. It's the same for Professor Sprout. She is always there to help when needed but keeps out of school drama otherwise. In a completely literary sense, she doesn't make a huge impact on the story. But in her individual students' lives, however, the biggest influence is seen.

✻ ACCEPTING ✻

Hogwarts was founded by four great witches and wizards. We learn pieces of Hogwarts' beginning from the Sorting Hat in *Goblet of Fire*:

> *Now each of these four founders*
> *Formed their own Houses, for each*
> *Did value different virtues*
> *In the ones they had to teach.*
> *By Gryffindor, the bravest were*
> *Prized far beyond the rest;*
> *For Ravenclaw, the cleverest*
> *Would always be the best;*
> ***For Hufflepuff, hard workers were***
> ***Most worthy of admission;***
> *And power-hungry Slytherin*
> *Loved those of great ambition.* [2]

As the series became more popular we began to take sides. We picked our houses, we wore the scarves and ties. Pottermore developed a sorting quiz and we all rushed to make it official. Our results just had to align with the house we had chosen from the very beginning.

When I first took the Pottermore quiz, I cheated. It was easy to identify which character trait went with each house. The Sorting Hat takes your choice into account so it's not really cheating, right? I was in Gryffindor! Just like our heroes of the story. I knitted a red and yellow scarf. I went to the movie premieres dressed in my house robes. Of course I was a Gryffindor.

But feelings of guilt began to wash over me. Was I being true to myself? Deep down I felt I truly belonged in Ravenclaw because of my love of learning. Heck, I'm a teacher! So I created a new Pottermore account and took the quiz again. I became nervous. There was no way I'd be placed in Slytherin, but what if I was in Hufflepuff? I felt like a first year about to put the Sorting Hat on my head in front of the whole school. I forced myself to answer each question honestly. It was hard. I contemplated each one. It was taking me so long I would certainly be considered a Hat Stall. Which road tempts me? The wide, sunny, grassy lane? The twisting, leaf-strewn path through woods? After agonizing over each question, I finally hit the button... and up popped red and yellow colors. I was shocked. I was actually sorted into Gryffindor. My fear of being in Hufflepuff was unnecessary and irrational.

I read a comment once that said if Helga Hufflepuff isn't your favorite founder, then you're wrong. They have a point, as an educator I do respect and admire Helga Hufflepuff's desire to teach all students no matter their background. The Sorting Hat elaborates on the founders' motivation in *Order of the Phoenix:*

> *United by a common goal,*
> *They had the selfsame yearning,*
> *To make the world's best magic school*
> *And pass along their learning.*
>
> ...
>
> *Said Slytherin, "We'll teach just those*
> *Whose ancestry is purest."*
> *Said Ravenclaw, "We'll teach those whose*
> *Intelligence is surest."*
> *Said Gryffindor, "We'll teach all those*
> *With brave deeds to their name,"*

Said Hufflepuff, "I'll teach the lot,
And treat them just the same."

...

For instance, Slytherin
Took only pure-blood wizards
Of great cunning, just like him,
And only those of sharpest mind
Were taught by Ravenclaw
While the bravest and boldest
Went to Gryffindor.
Good Hufflepuff, she took the rest,
And taught them all she knew[3]

These founders were the first teachers in the magical world, or at least the first we know about. As they were developing their plan for a new school, they each had in mind the type of students they wanted to educate. Salazar Slytherin put the protection of wizardkind first but in the process labeled an entire group of students as outcasts. Rowena Ravenclaw's desire to teach the smartest is similar to our university systems today. Colleges require students to pass tests and receive certain marks in order to move on. Godric Gryffindor is a little harder for me to place. Why would you only want to teach the brave? Sounds more like recruitment for a military school. Each of these other houses focus on a certain subset of students.

For this reason it is Helga Hufflepuff that is the true revolutionary. Even one thousand years ago, she chooses to include every single student, whether they are worthy or intelligent or brave or something else entirely. She wants to provide an education for everyone. I want to be this teacher. All great teachers believe they can provide a positive influence for every single student that walks through their door, no matter their race, abilities or confidence.

The greatest demonstration of Professor Sprout's welcoming embrace of each student is the relationship she fosters with Neville Longbottom.

Neville traipses around Hogwarts constantly feeling like an outcast, unwanted and unsuccessful. Professor Snape bullies him. Professor Trelawney points out his clumsiness. He makes a fool of himself in front of everyone in Madam Hooch's first flying lesson. He believes the heir of Slytherin is going to attack him for having so little magic in him. Even in Professor McGonagall's class he feels insecure and nervous.

But when he walks into the greenhouse with Professor Sprout, he is a different person. His demeanor changes entirely. He is confident, successful, and presented as an example. This is remarkable. Teachers like Lupin and Moody have been kind to Neville, but he was never successful in their classes, not like this. What does Professor Sprout do to help him feel comfortable? Having a love of plants certainly helped him progress in Herbology, but there is something extra that Professor Sprout brings to her relationship with Neville in the periphery that helps him thrive in her class.

One year I had a student who was hard of hearing. He was a great student and did every single assignment asked of him. But I felt so disconnected from him. I was communicating with him through an interpreter and while he was used to this, I wasn't satisfied. I looked up sign language basics online and became familiar with a few essential words and phrases. One day when he handed me the microphone that connected to his hearing aide, I signed thank you. He was ecstatic and his face lit up. It made my day thinking about how happy he was. At the end of class when I walked over and gave the microphone back, he signed thank you. The interpreter tried to speak his words aloud, but Carlos waved her off excitedly telling her I already knew what he was saying. I looked at him and said, "I am trying to learn some more but it's hard without someone to help. Can you show me how to say you're welcome?" The interpreter signed to him. Then he looked at me and slowly cupped his hand and moved it in a downward motion out from his chin then back towards his chest. I mirrored his motion and he smiled and nodded his head. From this point on he would teach me a new hand sign once a week and test me at the beginning of class the next day. Carlos and I even began to communicate on our own without the interpreter; I jokingly told her one day that we don't need you anymore. This system wasn't easy, and sometimes we had to write things down, but I loved that I could develop that relationship with him. After that moment, he would always stop me around campus to say hello.

Looking up sign language on Youtube was effective, but having Carlos teach me a new sign was much more natural. I felt I was able to connect with him in a way I initially didn't think was possible. At the end of the school year, right after the final bell rang, Carlos came up to me and told me that he loved being in my class, and that I was funny. In so few words he managed to remind me how much the extra effort I put into my class was worth it. Carlos would have been one of those students who moved on with little involvement. He'd be one of many forgotten faces that have passed through my classes and I would just be an insignificant memory to him. But going out of my way to understand him allowed me to connect with him on a deeper level.

Admittedly we can't have these connections with all of our students, but it's always worth the effort to try. Another year I had a seventh grade boy who would dress in the same black pants and black t-shirt every day. On the days that I actually could get him to work it was obvious that he was smart and knew history. Most days, however, he just sat there doodling and would explode in my face if I asked him to accomplish even the smallest task.

He was really obsessed with Jeff the Killer. I didn't know or care about this serial killer guy in the least, and I found it a bit disturbing that he knew so much about whatever it was. His goal in life was to catch this Jeff character. I guess that is better than wanting to be like him. He kept asking me if I knew anything about Jeff the Killer and I would always respond with no, but I'll look into it. While I had no desire to look this killer up, it seemed to make him happy in the moment.

One night, as I was laying in bed unable to sleep, I remembered his request. I pulled up Google on my phone and typed in 'Jeff the Killer.' Bad mistake. Several pairs of bloodshot eyes, set-in scarred white faces with blood red smiling lips were staring back at me. My eyes were darting every which way, heart skipping a beat. I frantically dropped the phone on to my chest, screen falling face down into the folds of the blanket, making the room pitch dark again. I was horrified. I took a deep breath and quickly closed out the browser while squinting my eyes in order to see less of the images again. The squinting didn't help much and I couldn't sleep the rest of the night.

What was I thinking? I lived alone and here I was googling serial killers from bed. Here's the Wikipedia entry I read the next morning:

> Jeff the Killer is a story accompanied by an image of the character. The story says that a teenager named Jeff was severely injured in an incident of bullying that caused his face to become burned. Following the incident, Jeff went insane and cut a smile into his cheeks and burned off his eyelids. He is now a serial killer who sneaks into houses at night and whispers "go to sleep" before murdering his victims. [4]

AHHHH! It still creeps me out. Why is my poor seventh grade boy following an internet horror-legend?

The next day Brandon was slouching in his chair in the front row and drawing absentmindedly on the corner of the handout I had just given him when I finally built up the courage to talk to him. "Hey, Brandon... So... I finally looked up Jeff the Killer last night." His face lit up instantaneously.

The student who was often grumpy, angry and downright nasty to everyone around him, was grinning ear to ear at the mere mention of this serial killer. I was taken aback. How do you respond to that? He rambled on for a few minutes about how he believes it's all true and wants to catch him. I tried to tell him it was all a cult following, but he dismissed this. I admitted to him that it freaked me out, and he simply laughed, but when I asked him to get to work, he actually did. I had to deal with Jeff the Killer updates once a week for the rest of the year, but I was finally able to break through that tough exterior and begin to form a relationship with him. It was a weird, often depressing relationship, but he did much better in my class after that moment. All it took was me googling for 3 minutes (and losing a full night of sleep), but it was worth it.

From what we see of their relationship, I have no doubt that Professor Sprout went out of her way to connect with Neville and make him feel comfortable in this same manner. When Neville receives a Mimbulus Mimbletonia for his birthday, he can't wait to show Professor Sprout. This enthusiasm isn't just about their shared love of plants. I imagine Professor Sprout welcoming him into the greenhouse during her office hours and talking about both plants and life while discovering properties that the Mimbulus Mimbletonia has to offer together.

However, connecting with the Nevilles of the world is much easier than developing relationships with the Dracos. In *Half-Blood Prince*, Malfoy doesn't trust anyone and is determined to stay alive at all costs, even initiating multiple failed murder attempts out of fear of Voldemort. Professor Snape is the only one who attempts to help him (on Dumbledore's orders), but this just pushes him further away. This is where our job becomes difficult. It's easy to care for those we understand and are most like us, but it is also our responsibility to care for the most off-putting, disconcerting, Jeff-the-killer-obsessed students.

We never see Professor Sprout interacting with Draco in this manner, but I get the sense that she goes out of her way to avoid playing favorites. While Neville is clearly the all-star of the group, he never receives undeserved house points. Hermione answers most of the questions, but isn't treated any better than Ron. And Harry is not given preferential treatment over Ernie McMillan because of his fame. If Professor Sprout was aware of Draco's issues, I'm sure she made attempts to console him. In this class, each student is accepted and equal and they thrive because of it.

* COLLABORATIVE *

Another key characteristic of Professor Sprout's teaching style is her willingness to work in collaboration with those around her. We see her accompany Slughorn to the greenhouse at twilight so he can pick leaves to use in his Potions classes. She also provides supplies to Madam Pompfrey like the mandrakes used to heal petrified students and bubotuber pus to help treat acne. Do you think Madam Pompfrey and Professor Sprout are friends? Do they eat lunch together? Maybe they discuss the needs of the infirmary and Professor Sprout plans her lessons around them. It would be a great way to incorporate real world applications into her lessons (well, real for them). Students would be able to understand at an even deeper level why it's important to know how to maintain these magical plants.

One of her most memorable lessons takes place in Chamber of Secrets when she teaches students how to repot Mandrakes. She gets them involved in a discussion on the Mandrake's properties, warns students that the plant's cries could knock them out for several hours if they remove their earmuffs and models the repotting. Only then does she release them to work with the baby Mandrakes in groups of four, ensuring they are ready. This is a successful hands-on lesson and the students learn a lot from this group activity.

This collaborative style is the only type of teaching we see occurring in Professor Sprout's classroom. The students never work alone, constantly tackling problems in a group of three or more. I am a firm believer in collaborative work. I'll often plan lessons like group posters, projects, and Socratic seminars. Learning to work through problems together helps students develop a skill set that they can carry on with them later in life.

One day I was telling my friend, Tori, about a Socratic seminar I had my students complete. She asked me if I was able to get everyone to talk. I actually did and I was proud of it, despite half the students only saying a couple of words to fulfill a mandatory part of their grade. I told her that I was honest with my students and explained that I am naturally introverted and don't like speaking in front of others either, but I still manage to do it every day for my job. When I told her about the Socratic seminar she insightfully said, "So... you make them do something you hate?" We both laughed and I said, "Yeah," but her words stuck with me. Was I putting too much emphasis on collaborative time? She's right, as a student I loved listening to lectures and hated being forced to work with others.

In Susan Cain's *Quiet* she writes that at least one-third of the world's population are introverts, yet extroverted qualities remain favored in most business circles. Someone who can give illuminating presentations is often valued over someone who does good analytical work at their desk. [5] Schools are beginning to value these virtues as well. We are encouraged to require presentations and group work. While introverts are very capable of doing this type of work, they thrive better on their own.

I am a perfect example of this, I need time to process information. I like to research and contemplate a lesson plan before sharing it with my coworkers. Tori is the opposite, she adapts quickly to working with others and can make immediate decisions on the spot. Because of my inability to do the same, we had to find a balance between our two personalities. Without specifically addressing our differences, she recognized this need and changed how our planning meetings were run. Now, she often comes up with an idea and hands me a hard copy to review or she'll call, pose a question and then tell me to call her back with my thoughts. This gives me time to process alone before returning with changes and ideas.

If I need this type of adjustment working with someone who I am already comfortable with, then what type of adjustments should I allow for my own students? Was I really helping them? Getting the best from them?

This challenged the way I structured group work. While I still think it is necessary and important, I sometimes provide alternative assignments for students who are naturally more introverted. Now, when planning Socratic seminars I give my students the option of writing an essay instead of participating in the discussion. This way students are challenged to the best of their abilities without suffering through an unsuitable work style. I need to remember to cultivate the ones who have a temperament similar to my own. There needs to be a balance.

It isn't clear if Professor Sprout ever has her students work individually. When they leave Hogwarts and move into their homes all across the countryside they will often be facing magical plants on their own. Will they be able to tackle them alone? Or will they need those three other group members to repot a mandrake, extract bubotuber pus or to interact with any number of crazy plants waiting in their new garden?

Professor Sprout is a great teacher, but if she doesn't give them time to practice these skills on their own they might be unsuccessful when dealing with magical plants in their own lives. Perhaps we're only privileged to her collaborative work because that's more interesting to read about or maybe individual work isn't focused on until later years. Professor Sprout often has students' best interests in mind, so I'm sure she has her own ways of holding each student accountable and balances her lessons between individual and collaborative work ensuring every student has the chance to be successful.

∗ ∗ ∗

Professor Sprout is the type of teacher I would have felt comfortable turning to for guidance as a shy high school student or in my beginning years of teaching. I was often in need of a mentor who was willing to help, no questions asked. Hufflepuffs value hard work, patience, loyalty and fair play. We see no greater example of these characteristics than Professor Sprout. She goes out of her way to work in collaboration with other staff members and helps disadvantaged students from all backgrounds become successful at Hogwarts.

After Dumbledore's death, she is the first one to speak up in defense of the students, suggesting, *"I feel that if a single pupil wants to come, then the school ought to remain open for that pupil."*[6] The dedicated work of Hufflepuffs like Professor Sprout should never be considered a demonstration of weakness, but one of true strength. Open-minded and kindhearted, Professor Sprout embodies the qualities of a truly caring teacher, something we should all try to emulate. I'm sure Helga Hufflepuff would be proud to see her carry on these welcoming traditions as Head of Hufflepuff House.

PROFESSOR FLITWICK

INTERACTIVE * PASSIONATE

"Oh, well done!" cried Professor Flitwick, clapping. "Everyone see here, Miss Granger's done it!"[1]

HEAD OF RAVENCLAW * CHARMS

In the Charms classroom, students learn to change an object's basic purpose by silencing ravens and making pineapples tap-dance. In this class, objects frequently fly across the room while a small man stands at the back, smiling at his students and shouting, *"Well done!"* Perhaps Professor Flitwick has been hit with too many stray Cheering Charms over the years, but it seems as if nothing ever phases him. Even when Professor Umbridge is going around firing teachers in *Order of the Phoenix*, Flitwick is said to have *"Treated her like a guest."*[2] I can't make it a week without getting frustrated with students' lack of interest and annoyed by their need for repeated instructions. But Flitwick seems to have limitless amounts of energy that propel him through the day. As Head of Ravenclaw House, perhaps it is his love of learning that keeps his passion at high levels. He is the teacher I try to channel at the end of the day when my cup feels empty, both literally and figuratively (caffeinated tea is my secret to survival). Professor Flitwick is consistently animated, patient and encouraging which is exactly what students need in a school of magic.

✳ INTERACTIVE ✳

Over the course of six years, students learn a variety of charms in Flitwick's class including levitation, summoning, cheering, silencing and even how to turn vinegar into wine. These are all practical skills students can use in the magical world outside of Hogwarts. Sure, teaching students to create alcohol probably isn't the best idea, but any working adult won't deny the spell's usefulness.

In Harry's first year, students learn to levitate objects using Wingardium Leviosa. Flitwick first models the spell for students, has them practice the proper *"swish and flick"* wrist movement, and then reminds them to say the spell correctly. He provides a real life example as to why this is important, saying, *"Never forget Wizard Baruffio, who said 's' instead of 'f' and found himself on the floor with a buffalo on his chest."*[3] Later, when Hermione's life is being threatened by an overzealous troll, Wingardium Leviosa is the first spell to form in Ron's mind. Thanks to proper training, he manages to perform the swish and flick movement and pronounce the charm correctly, saving his friend's life.

Flitwick's interactive class structure means students are never required to sit and listen to him speak for long periods of time. In *Prisoner of Azkaban*, even though Harry and Ron are only a few minutes late to a lesson on Cheering Charms, Flitwick already has his students divided into pairs practicing the spell, suggesting he rarely wastes class time on drawn out instructions.

Because of this commotion, however, Harry, Ron and Hermione are able to avoid notice and hold private discussions. Even though they don't always use their time effectively, it is not for lack of effort on Flitwick's part. Throughout his classes, he constantly patrols the room. At one point when Harry and Ron are deep in conversation, Flitwick walks over to them, commenting, *"Now, now, boys…A little less talk, a little more action… Let me see you try…"*[4] When they fail to perform the charm, Flitwick reminds them to stay on task and assigns extra practice as homework. Even when Ron accidentally messes up the charm for turning vinegar into wine and shards of glass fly at Professor Flitwick he doesn't revert to simple textbook work. He just tells Ron to keep trying and to practice more for homework.

I want my students to have this same opportunity to practice skills within a classroom setting. So one year, I had them participate in a Meeting of the Minds discussion about who really discovered America. Before the discussion I had students prepare by watching a video and reading excerpts on a specific explorer they were assigned. One student asked, "Why do we have to do this if you already know the answer?" All this research and speculation, in her opinion, was too much work. Before I could respond, another student said, "Because they don't know the answer." The first student replied, "So why don't we just keep saying Christopher Columbus?" Another student stood up and shouted, "How can you f—ing say that when you have just seen all this evidence that more people were here before him?! I'm not going to give him credit anymore!"

After this confrontation I was nervous to hand the discussion over to my class. I tried to get them really excited about the conference using Alan Rickman-like pauses for added suspense. "Tomorrow… we will get a chance to hear from these explorers. They are traveling through time… and space… to be here with us. Make sure you come up with some really good questions to ask them and we'll finally figure out who *reallyyyy* discovered America."

The next day I had students running into my classroom asking "Where is he?" At first I was confused, then I remembered they thought Columbus was coming to class that day. It's amazing what junior high students will believe.

The rest of the class came in and sat down. Some were excited, others were nervous, but everyone was attentive. I explained to them that one member of each group will take on the role of their explorer and try to prove that they were the first to truly discover America. To my relief, they seemed intrigued at the prospect. I had the speakers sit at tables in the center of the room with their name placards in front of them. I welcomed everyone to our Explorers Conference and thanked the explorers for traveling so far through time and space to be with us. I then explained the rules, making sure to highlight the difference between a debate and an argument.

With a little trepidation, I relinquished the controls and let the students take over the discussion. I should never have been worried. They did a great job embodying their explorers and backed everything they said with evidence. When we had completed our discussion, a boy who was known for fidgeting and getting distracted proclaimed loudly, "awww...it's like watching TV."

If done well, this kind of activity is a great way to get students involved in the learning process. I had students on the outside of the circle take notes while those inside discuss. Students then took turns inside the circle so they could also practice their speaking and listening skills. While it was nerve-racking to give students all the power, just like in Flitwick's class, all it took was a small bit of guidance for them to take learning into their own hands.

Flitwick also knows when it's not worth battling students on certain matters. In *Goblet of Fire*, as the end of the term nears and the highly anticipated Yule Ball approaches, he allows the students to play games in his class. What type of games do you play in a class where students are already allowed to send objects flying across the room? At this point it is unlikely that any of them will be focused enough to learn new coursework, so this is for the best. I should have followed his example when I tried to hold a Socratic seminar on imperialism… on Halloween. Students dressed as a bunny, a clown or an emoji just can't be taken seriously.

It is important to remember that some things are out of our control. Interactive lessons help students get excited about learning and coming to school. These activities, however, can quickly become chaotic if not planned out well, making teachers wary of handing over control of their class. Flitwick shows us that chaos can be channeled into effective learning through constant observation and sincere encouragement. When life-threatening situations arise, his students are able to perform reliably because of the practice they have had in a classroom full of conversations, stray spells and explosions. If we give our students a little more freedom and have high expectations for them, they will rise up to the challenge.

❋ PASSIONATE ❋

Flitwick may be small in stature, but he has a large personality. His enthusiasm and passion rival a niffler's love of shiny objects. It is his passion for his students and love of learning that gives him the energy needed to plan interactive lessons every day.

In Harry's first Charms lesson, Flitwick is standing on a pile of books and gets so excited that he topples out of sight. In high school I had a teacher who was so passionate about history that he would lean all the way forward on his tiptoes when he became excited. It looked like his brain was top heavy with information that was desperate to come spilling out. Every Friday he would give an extra credit quiz pertaining to current events. He was tip-toe-passionate about history, but he loved raisins even more. Each week a question about the sun-dried grape would pop up in-between facts about major world events. It was this quirky passion that helped me connect with him more than my other teachers that year.

Professor Flitwick's passion makes him one of the most encouraging and positive teachers at Hogwarts. He goes out of his way to inspire and motivate students. We see this in many moments throughout the series.

In *Sorcerer's Stone* when Hermione successfully levitates her feather, he claps his hands and comments *"Oh, well done! ... Everyone see here, Miss Granger's done it!"*[5] When Fred and George create a swamp in the hallway to rebel against Umbridge, Flitwick is so proud that he ropes it off and leaves it as a tribute to their excellent spell work. Imagine the number of years and the number of students Flitwick has taught. How old is he, anyway? No matter his age, his enthusiasm hasn't wavered one bit. He is just as excited for Hermione on her first successful attempt at Wingardium Leviosa as he is when she successfully silences her raven in her fifth year.

I find it hard to be passionate like this every day, but bringing passion into my lessons is always worth it. While discussing the way slaves were auctioned on cinder blocks, I stood on a stool to emphasize the vulnerability they would have felt while slaveowners were analyzing their value like a piece of meat. My students were shocked to see me do something so out of the ordinary. They couldn't keep their eyes off me. Maybe they were hoping I would topple out of sight like Flitwick, but either way, they were all engaged and listening.

When I teach students about the French Revolution I have students take on societal roles from that time period. The boy and girl with the highest grades become king and queen for the day. I crown their heads, let them sit in my comfortable office chairs and lay out a red carpet (really just a red table cloth from the dollar store). Then to top it off, they each get a ring pop because everyone knows royalty need expensive jewelry to demonstrate their social status. They are excused from the day's notes, later provided with a printed copy, and get to enjoy watching their kingdom work.

The rest of the students pick from a deck of cards I have created that say lord, lady, knight, or peasant. They are assigned seats based on their social status: lords and ladies in the front, knights in the second row, and peasants are forced to sit in the back. This activity is designed to help my students understand the feudal system. I split a large bag of M&Ms which represent the crop yield amongst the social classes. We simulate the 'crops' moving from the peasants all the way to the king and queen. At the end of the day, peasants have the least amount and royalty have the most.

This process is very interactive but I still have to manage complaints throughout the class period, especially when I purposefully provoke the peasants by talking down to them. I make sure to compliment the king and queen and give them treats throughout the entire period. One year I even paused the lesson and popped a bag of popcorn just for them. The peasants, who only got five M&Ms, were outraged. It was easy for them to make the connection as to why the real peasants during the French Revolution would revolt against the monarchy and the estate system.

This activity takes time to prepare and it only works with a class of students who trust you. But my passion for their learning shines through in these lessons. That and it's hard not to enjoy the look of despair on the peasants' faces as their hard-earned M&Ms are handed to the king and queen. They may not remember every detail about the French Revolution, but they do remember the effort I put into engaging them.

There are other ways to show our students we are passionate about our job that don't take as much time. Flitwick puts up fairy lights around Christmas time to add extra charm to his classroom. In my own class, when my students give a speech about who they feel is most influential in U.S. History, I let them use the podium and project a GIF of a waving American flag in the background. It looks spectacular and makes the students feel empowered. And when I simulate the feel of assembly line work, I put on factory sounds I find on Youtube and shut off the lights to add to the effect. Each of these scenarios cost me little money and time, but my students appreciated the lesson so much more because of the extra effort put in to make it a special day.

Robert L. Fried, author of *The Passionate Teacher*, explains that passionate teachers are ones who enter the classroom because they love kids. But passion isn't just a benefit for our students, "It is also a gift we give ourselves: a way of honoring our life's work, our profession. It says: 'I know why I am devoting this life I've got to these children.'[6] Fried outlines two main observations of passionate teachers: 1) Passionate teachers get at the heart of their subject and share the beauty of what drew them to the subject in the first place and 2) Passionate teachers show their passion by partnering in learning with students.[7] Professor Flitwick embodies both these characteristics to become a truly passionate teacher.

We are all passionate about something and when this passion transfers into our classroom our students notice. It ignites their curiosity and gets them excited about our subject matter. I also find that when my students are excited to enter my classroom and learn, my job is much more enjoyable. At the end of the year I have my students fill out a reflection form and one of the questions is 'Who has had the greatest impact on your life this year?' "Ms. Dickie," an eighth grade boy who was often bullied in the locker room and had an abusive home life wrote. I was touched, and then I read on. With one sentence he was able to simplify my entire teaching philosophy: "because she told her story and made history our story."

When I think of influential Hogwarts professors, Flitwick is one that jumps to the top of the list. He is consistently available and solidly dependable while the wizarding world rapidly changes around them. Despite only seeing him in the classroom a few times, his impact is widely seen. His passion for the subject and his students are what we remember, leaving an influence that goes beyond the number of pages devoted to him. The same can be said of Muggle teachers. If we can share our passion for teaching with our students, they will remember this more than any history fact, math formula or poem.

PROFESSOR MCGONAGALL

STRICT * CONSCIENTIOUS * RESPECTED

"Transfiguration is some of the most complex and dangerous magic you will learn at Hogwarts... Anyone messing around in my class will leave and not come back."[1]

HEAD OF GRYFFINDOR * TRANSFIGURATION

Professor McGonagall serves as Transfiguration teacher every year that Harry attends Hogwarts. In her class, students are taught to transfigure matches to needles, beetles into buttons, and teapots into tortoises. These enchantments may come across as inconsequential in comparison to other spells they're learning. Even if I desperately needed a pincushion, it's not like I have an extra hedgehog roaming my spare bedroom ready to be transformed. McGonagall, however, uses these basic skills as preparation for actual human transfiguration which they begin in their sixth year. I wonder if teaching human transfiguration causes extra headaches for McGonagall as she combats Colin Creevey's lightning bolt-shaped mohawk and Luna Lovegood's lion updo. Is there a dress code enforced at

Hogwarts? I know students are required to wear robes, but what about hair color and length? Perhaps she allows this frivolity and appreciates the complex spell-work behind their embellished looks, just as Flitwick was proud of the twins' portable swamp. Knowing her propensity for keeping Hogwarts in order, however, I'm sure in more rambunctious cases she points her wand at these experimental students and quickly returns their hair to its normal, unimaginative state.

Harry's first impression of Professor McGonagall, even before he learns she can transform herself into an animal, is that she *"was not someone to cross."*[2] She's described as a *"stern looking witch who wore her hair in a tight bun"*[3] and is one of the strictest, most dedicated teachers at Hogwarts. By Harry's first year, she has already devoted herself to this profession for over thirty-four years! She embodies the Gryffindor trait of courage, fitting for the Head of its House, but she is also caring, ambitious and intelligent—traits the other three houses value most. In McGonagall's classroom, everyone has the chance to succeed if they are willing to put in the effort.

∗ STRICT ∗

No matter which house students belong, Professor McGonagall has the same high expectations for them all. Her class is considered one of the most rigorous on campus, a sentiment shared by McGonagall who must remind students that they cannot be successful with their minds *"on their dinner."*[4] Even with the most difficult tasks, she expects students to work hard and perform at high levels.

In Harry's second year, as McGonagall tells her class that their tests would take place in two weeks, they explode with questions. Many thought that with a monster on the loose, exams would be canceled. But McGonagall has other plans and explains, *"The whole point of keeping the school open at this time is for you to receive your education."*[5] Even with an unknown petrifier loose in the castle, McGonagall still expects her students to study diligently for their tests. McGonagall also begins preparing them for their O.W.L.s in their fourth year even though they won't take these exams until the end of their fifth. And when Harry's fifth year begins, her O.W.L. speech becomes even fiercer, saying, *"You cannot pass an O.W.L....without serious application, practice and study."*[6]

She has the same high expectations when it comes to behavior she tolerates around Hogwarts. Harry describes her as having the ability to *"spot trouble quicker than any teacher in the school."* In *Sorcerer's Stone,* McGonagall introduces her class by saying *"Anyone messing around in my class will leave and not come back. You have been warned."*[7] She makes it clear from day one that she will not tolerate any rule breaking. Throughout the series we see her follow through countless times.

When Hermione tells McGonagall she went looking for the troll in her first year, McGonagall takes five points away. Hermione is in McGonagall's house and is top of the class. She's teary eyed and has just been attacked by a fully-grown mountain troll, but that doesn't stop McGonagall from punishing her.

Later in *Sorcerer's Stone,* when Professor McGonagall catches Harry and Hermione up in the astronomy tower, she takes fifty points from each of them. Always impartial, she also takes points from Malfoy, who reported the other two, and Neville, who only gets out of bed to warn them. And when they try to get to the third floor corridor to stop the Sorcerer's Stone from being taken, she threatens them with taking fifty more points from Gryffindor. Ron is shocked but McGonagall simply says, *"Yes, Weasley, from my own house!"*[8] No matter which house students belong, if they break a rule, they will have consequences.

In *Prisoner of Azkaban,* Harry desperately wants to visit Hogsmeade, but he doesn't have a signed permission slip. It could have been really easy for McGonagall to allow him. She knows about Harry's abusive home life and despises the Dursleys for their treatment of Harry. Even though it's fairly ridiculous that students can play Quidditch, brew dangerous potions and work with menacing beasts without permission, it is a school rule. She doesn't waiver and makes him stay in the castle, telling him *"The form clearly states the parent or guardian must give permission....I'm sorry, Potter, but that's my final word."*[9] These moments may seem inconsequential, but they prove Professor Mcgonagall's consistency above all else, even if she disappoints her students in the process. No matter how small the misbehavior or decision, she makes sure they acknowledge their mistakes and learn from them.

I always start the school year with high expectations of the behavior and activities I will allow in my classroom such as not allowing students to have their cellphones out. Yet, as the school year progresses things get worse and worse. One student has a phone out, but they're looking up a word they don't know, so I allow it. The next week they have it out, but their mom is texting them. Then it's all downhill from there. Soon, every student has their phone out and it's nearly impossible to combat. By this point it is too late to fix. If I was consistent every single day, then I wouldn't have as big of a cellphone problem. But I let it slide too many times. I try to tell myself that my job is to educate students, not to constantly tell them to put their phones away, but the reality of teaching is I have to be both a teacher and an enforcer. I need to remember that, like Professor McGonagall demonstrates, consistency is key to any good classroom structure.

Even in Professor McGonagall's thirty-eighth year, she manages to constantly maintain order in her classroom. As the bell is about to ring and Harry and Ron take out fake wands for a sword fight, she shouts at them to pay attention. Even at the end of class, with all supplies put away, she still expects students to be listening. After quickly getting their attention, she makes an announcement about the Yule Ball. This instance seems to be one of the rare moments of down time in Professor McGonagall's class. While Professor Flitwick lets students play games at the end of term, McGonagall keeps her students working up to the last minute.

The last five minutes of class are my least favorite. I hate that glossed-over, I-just-want-to-reach-for-my-bag-and-shove-things-into-it kind of look students give as they anticipate leaving. I'm not sure why they start packing up so early, it's not like they have to pack for a distant vacation in a foreign land. They walk several yards away just to get the same supplies out again. Now that I teach high school, my students are usually mature enough to finish our lesson a minute or two early and sit patiently for the bell. But when I taught junior high, it was as if they had transformed into Blast-Ended Skrewts. On days they were particularly restless, I would let them pack up their things a few minutes early then put on a Youtube video. This eliminated the stress of sword fights occurring in the back of my classroom and allowed us a moment to bond over whatever motivational or humorous videos I had recently discovered.

Professor McGonagall makes her strict teaching philosophy clear when Umbridge attempts to interrupt her lesson during an evaluation. She vehemently tells her, "*I do not generally permit people to talk when I'm talking.*"[10] In fact, McGonagall rarely has discipline problems in her class because of her rigid management. But at the same time, she knows the best way to eliminate misbehavior, no matter the cause, is to have engaging curriculum. When students are bored in class, they act out. In her class, there is no down time for students to misbehave. Similar to Professor Flitwick, she is constantly monitoring the room and providing difficult spell work to practice, keeping them focused at all times. Her rigorous lessons and consistent management of misbehaviors are what make her successful in the classroom.

✳ CONSCIENTIOUS ✳

Consistency is important when dealing with misbehavior, but it is just as important to understand why our students act out. Professor McGonagall has great classroom management because she doesn't randomly punish students or blankly assign detention for all abuses. She gets to know her students, advises them and helps correct their behavior.

In *Sorcerer's Stone*, she pulls Harry out of his flying lesson immediately after he disobeys Madam Hooch's directive to stay on the ground. Harry thinks he's going to be expelled, rightly so as he was swiftly breaking the rules. Instead, she finds a constructive outlet for his flying abilities. She secures a spot for him as seeker and now he belongs to a team where he has to train, prepare and be responsible. How much better is this than sitting him in detention for a week?

I had a seventh grade boy who hated everything about school and was in detention every other day. The only thing he truly enjoyed was drawing pictures. The problem was, he was particularly fond of drawing a specific girl's head attached to a horse's body. I tried desperately to get him to stop. I had serious discussions with him about the way he was treating people and even had him suspended for bullying. It seemed there would be no end to his abuse, until one day I decided to give him the option of drawing responses to some tasks instead of writing. Once I found an outlet for his skill, his inappropriate pictures circulated less frequently.

McGonagall demonstrates her conscientious decisions again when Harry is accused of petrifying Mrs. Norris. Snape wants him taken off the Gryffindor Quidditch team, but McGonagall steps in and says, *"I see no reason to stop the boy playing Quidditch. This cat wasn't hit over the head with a broomstick."*[11] Logically, it makes sense not to take away students' extra-curricular activities as punishment. Sometimes this is the only thing keeping them focused in school. But punishment in schools isn't always logical. Even McGonagall makes this mistake. When she catches Harry, Hermione, Malfoy and Neville out of bed their first year, she assigns them detention in the Forbidden Forest—after hours. McGonagall, what were you thinking? Having students run around in search of a murdered unicorn in a dark, *forbidden* forest is clearly a bad idea.

When I first started teaching there were so many students late to class that my administration implemented a new tardy policy. For every period students were late, they were required to serve detention at lunch or after school for thirty minutes. I'm glad they were attempting to fix the problem, but students just stopped attending detention. So administration took it to the next step. They would send campus assistants around to the classes to pick up all the students who had detention. Not only were they pulling out students twenty to thirty minutes early from class, students would often get "lost" along the way. We were attempting to punish students, but they were missing more class time because of detention than they ever did when they were just late. Punishments like this put the pressure and responsibility on the teacher or administration to correct the problem. Instead, we should have focused more of our effort on consequences, which teach students that good and bad things happen in direct correlation with the choices we make. Teaching students why it's important to get to class on time would have gone a lot further than letting them miss class anyway for detention.

Discipline is one of the hardest things to manage in a classroom. Sometimes we have thirty-five students sitting in front of us, each with their own individual problems. We have to be understanding like McGonagall and realize that every student has a unique background and there may be a reason they are misbehaving.

Sometimes students come to us with problems outside of school. Neville's parents were tortured by one of Lord Voldemort's followers. They are alive, but mentally unstable. He lives with his grandmother who puts a lot of pressure on him to be something he is not. Neville is scared and nervous which causes him to underperform in school. His home life affects his ability to learn. He doesn't intentionally misbehave, but it does cause him to get in a few fights. When he fails to perform in Snape's class he is assigned detention, but in McGonagall's he is given extra practice and individual attention.

At my own school I see these problems daily. One day I walked into the front office and saw one of my students sitting there waiting to be sent home. When a teacher asked him to put his skateboard and slinky away during class he had refused. I just wanted to get my copies made quickly during my prep period but I stopped and took another look at him. I saw a tired, broken young boy who could do nothing but clench his slinky in his hands, sitting on his upside-down skateboard as if it might roll away at any moment. He trusted no one but himself.

Derek was homeless. He wore his P.E. clothes and the same dirty brown sweatshirt every day to school. His freckles and red hair helped mask the dirt on his skin, but just barely. Students complained that he smelled and didn't want to be seated by him. And these were the minor issues Derek had to deal with on a daily basis. As I talked to him, I realized that the skateboard and slinky were the only two things he truly owned. They were not the school's, they were not his friends', but his. If I only had two possessions in the world, one of them being my transportation, I wouldn't let go of them either.

Administration decided to give him a three day suspension for not handing over everything he owns in the world. Is this fair? Derek certainly thought it was worth it. But now he will not be in school where he is guaranteed food and warmth. I decided to make a deal with Derek. I told him that when he got back from his suspension, he should bring his skateboard and slinky straight to me. I'd let him store both items in my locked cabinet that nobody but myself has access to. This way he didn't have to carry it around all day and nobody will try to take it from him. Derek seemed generally excited to have a place to lock his stuff up and enthusiastically agreed. How much better is this than sending a kid home for wanting to keep his most prized possessions?

One of McGonagall's finest moments occurs when her teaching style comes into direct conflict with Umbridge's. In *Order of the Phoenix*, Professor Umbridge sends Harry out of her class for calling her a liar. McGonagall understands that Harry is not to blame in this situation, although she does caution him to stay calm in her presence. I absolutely love her response upon receiving the note from Umbridge:

> *"Is it true that you shouted at Professor Umbridge?"*
> *"Yes," said Harry.*
> *"You called her a liar?"*
> *"Yes."*
> *"You told her He-Who-Must-Not-Be-Named is back?"*
> *"Yes."*
> *Professor McGonagall sat down behind her desk, frowning at Harry. Then she said, "Have a biscuit, Potter."* [12]

Up to this point in the book Harry has felt ostracized by the wizarding community, by Dumbledore and even by his friends. His teacher has just called him a liar in front of his classmates and insulted someone who died right in front of him. The last thing Harry needs is for Professor McGonagall to yell at him or to assign him even more detentions. Instead, she treats him like a human, talks to him and cautions him—the response of a great teacher. Except for sending students on a nighttime stroll into the Forbidden Forest (I place more blame on plot than on McGonagall's personal mistake) she consistently makes fair and conscientious decisions when faced with student misbehavior.

✳ RESPECTED ✳

Professor McGonagall is highly respected by all students at Hogwarts, even among Gryffindor house's sheer enemies, the Slytherins. She earns this regard because of strict but fair classroom management combined with genuine respect for her students. Teachers that attempt to demand reverence through appearance or harsh language alone only succeed in gaining students' attention. In McGonagall's classroom, however, respect flows both ways, creating a more positive learning environment.

During Harry's first lesson in Transfiguration, McGonagall immediately has them work on transfiguring a match into a needle. Only

Hermione is able to make anything remotely silver or sharp, but instead of belittling the other students as Professor Snape often does, McGonagall focuses on the positive and gives her *"a rare smile."* [13] This is the first sense students get that there's more to their professor than her tight hair bun.

Despite her severe expressions and no-nonsense management system, there are many times in the series when McGonagall goes out of her way to help students. As Harry joins the Quidditch team, she convinces Dumbledore that he should be allowed a broomstick despite restrictions placed on first years. She even purchases him one of the most expensive brooms available. How much do Hogwarts professors actually make anyway?

She trusts Harry without hesitation. When he tells her he didn't put his name in the Goblet of Fire his fourth year and that he saw Mr. Weasley being attacked by a snake in his fifth, she stands by his side. I like to think I believe in my students, but if one of them came to me saying they dreamed about a giant snake and they thought it was real, I would laugh. I know they can all do magic, but that's some next level trust from McGonagall.

When she is helping students plan for their courses in their sixth year, she speaks up for Neville in the face of his grandmother's criticism, saying, *"It's high time your grandmother learned to be proud of the grandson she's got, rather than the one she thinks she ought to have —"* [14] While this may be the first compliment Professor McGonagall has given Neville, it is an important one. Neville can go on in his career choice knowing that Professor McGonagall, one of the strictest teachers at Hogwarts, has faith in him. And when Umbridge threatens to stop Harry's dream of becoming an Auror, McGonagall tells him, *"I will assist you to become an Auror if it is the last thing I do! If I have to coach you nightly I will make sure you achieve the required results!"* [15] McGonagall does everything within her power to help, protect and educate her students, and students look up to her because of it.

Professor McGonagall also gains student's respect by caring about their lives outside of the classroom and sharing her passion as, perhaps, Gryffindors' biggest Quidditch fan. She engages in conversation with many of the players and is often seen motivating the team before matches. As a former Gryffindor Quidditch member herself, this connection she has with students is great, but her willingness to support them after hours on the pitch is what makes students come to respect her even more. When she watches the games she gets so into the matches that when Lee Jordan is directing foul language at Malfoy for cheating, she doesn't even notice and begins shouting herself. Attending a student's match, concert or play is such a simple act that can go a long way. Whenever I attend these events, students feel a connection deeper than just my subject matter. It's one thing to tell your students you care about them, but the best way to show it is for them to see it with their own eyes.

These interactions, however, don't only take place at large sporting events. One day after school as I walked across the campus to my car, three of my students were playing with a soccer ball and it popped out in my direction. As a former soccer player, I automatically moved towards it and began to play with the ball at my feet. In one hand I was carrying my bag holding my laptop and in the other I had a box of candy.

I began to juggle the ball. Not my best demonstration of skill, mind you, because I was still in my nice work shoes. The ball dropped after a few times hitting it with both feet and one student said "you've got moves...let's see the rainbow." This, unfortunately, is not one of the skills in my repertoire. Instead of admitting this, I told them, "I don't want to drop my Nerds." They laughed and we parted ways. They loved every second of that small interaction and it only took a few minutes detour from my destination.

Professor McGonagall is also willing to share her sarcastic personality with her students and they respect her more for it. In *Prisoner of Azkaban*, Professor Trelawney made a prediction that Harry would soon have a tragic death. The rest of the third years are rattled when they walk into their next class lesson with Professor McGonagall, but Harry is downright despondent. McGonagall attempts to impress them with transfiguring herself into a cat, something they haven't seen yet and is a rare ability even in the magical world. She expects applause, but the class doesn't respond. Instead of simply moving on with her lesson, she discovers what is the matter and uses humor to bring students back to focus. She tells Harry, *"You look in excellent health to me, Potter, so you will excuse me if I don't let you off homework today, I assure you that if you die, you need not hand it in."*[16] This sarcastic comment is exactly what Harry needed to get him laughing and focused on the lesson again. He's no longer scared of a small pile of tea leaves, and the rest of the class has greater respect for McGonagall and her ability to laugh in the face of danger.

Professor McGonagall earns respect by caring for her students, taking an interest in their passions and sharing hers with them. But she keeps the respect of students and staff by being among the strictest, most consistent teachers at Hogwarts, all while maintaining her sense of integrity.

* * *

Professor McGonagall, like most teachers, doesn't get the credit she deserves. Dumbledore may be considered the wisest and most powerful wizard of all time, but it is McGonagall who helps keep even him focused and in line. When he tries to tell a bar joke in one of his opening speeches, it is her cleared throat that makes him reconsider. She is the one who stays behind to pick up the pieces when he's kicked out by the school governors, when he's on the run from Fudge and especially after his death. When both are asked to conjure chairs, Dumbledore produces a squashy, comfortable armchair. But Professor McGonagall conjures a rigid, wooden one—an accurate visual of the steadiness and strength she provides when Hogwarts needs it most.

Pottermore provides a detailed and intriguing description of Minerva

McGonagall's past. As a young girl she was a dedicated student and standout Quidditch player. She fell in and out of love, dealing with loss in a number of different ways. Nevertheless, these experiences don't affect her teaching ability. Professor McGonagall devotes herself to her profession and this can be seen in all aspects of her teaching. Her strict, unbiased form of classroom management helps students become successful not only in her classroom but also life outside of Hogwarts.

And it is the respect between her and her students that creates an environment where they can ask for help at any time. When Dumbledore says *"Help will always be given at Hogwarts to those who ask for it,"*[17] he probably means 'Go ask McGonagall.' She is such a constant in students' lives that when she is attacked by Umbridge and sent to St. Mungo's, Harry is astonished: *"he had always expected Professor McGonagall to be there, irascible and inflexible, perhaps, but always dependably, solidly present."*[18] Only a near death experience can keep Professor McGonagall from helping her students and because of this she should be remembered as one of Hogwarts' greatest teachers.

PROFESSOR SNAPE

ANTAGONISTIC * BULLY

"Moronic though some of this class undoubtedly are, I expect you to scrape an 'Acceptable' in your O.W.L., or suffer my... displeasure."[1]

HEAD OF SLYTHERIN * POTIONS * DEFENSE AGAINST THE DARK ARTS

Professor Snape is a highly intelligent and talented wizard. On paper he has all the qualifications necessary to make a good teacher, but in reality he is *"Cruel, sarcastic, and disliked by everybody except the students from his own house."*[2] An unpopular student at Hogwarts, Severus Snape was obsessed with the Dark Arts and was often antagonized by Harry's father. This resentment ingrained itself and transfers to Harry—his own student. After his Hogwarts education, he joins Lord Voldemort's ranks as a Death Eater until the only person he truly loves, Harry's mother, is killed at Voldemort's hand. In her memory, he aligns himself with Dumbledore, becomes a teacher, and does everything in his power to keep Harry alive—everything except teaching Harry the skills he needs to actually keep himself alive, that is. Even his love for Lily Potter can't stop him from belittling Harry at every opportunity. How much more successful would Harry have been if Snape had been compassionate rather than cruel?

For the purpose of this book, I will only examine Professor Snape as a teacher. I don't want us to forget that he is a complicated character with a dark past and a heroic future. For better and for worse, this shapes how he behaves inside and outside the classroom. We all have complicated lives and it's important to learn from Professor Snape's failures. Our personal issues shouldn't ruin our ability to connect with students as it does in Snape's dark, dingy classroom.

∗ ANTAGONISTIC ∗

Professor Snape is defined by all the things he is not. Slytherins value ambition, but as a Hogwarts professor, he lacks any desire to achieve. Perhaps as a Death Eater he was ambitious, but now he only passively performs his role at Hogwarts, resentful of his teaching position and his inability to become something greater.

As a teacher, he more closely resembles an irate Ravenclaw. He expects students to come into his class with prior knowledge they couldn't possibly learn without his help. On Harry's first day, he asks him to describe the functions of a bezoar. Until a few months ago Harry didn't even know how his parents died or that he was a wizard and now Snape is berating him for not knowing the use of an obscure magical object. He reminds me of college professors who were chosen for their intelligence and research, rather than their ability to interact with students. There is no doubt that he possesses the knowledge and skills of an accomplished potions master, but when it comes to teaching he acts as if every mistake a student makes spells irredeemable failure. When students are moving on to upper level N.E.W.T. classes, he will only accept students into his class who score the highest possible grade on the exams, an Outstanding. Despite these high standards, he remains a teacher unwilling to guide diverse students, a scholar reluctant to share his knowledge, and a strict authoritarian without a conscience.

As an introduction to Potions, Professor Snape begins with:

> *"You are here to learn the subtle science and exact art of potionmaking," ...He spoke in barely more than a whisper, but they caught every word — like Professor McGonagall, Snape had the gift of keeping a class silent without effort.* [3]

There are some teachers who have this immediate effect on students. They barely place a pinky toe in the class and everyone immediately falls silent. I wish I could demand attention like Snape. If I could just walk into a room and inspire fear in students, at least they would be quiet. One day, I was so fed up with my students not listening that I slammed my clipboard down on the edge of the desk and attempted to yell at the top of my lungs. But I got too emotional, my voice cracked half way through the scream, the words were unintelligible and the clipboard slipped out of my sweaty hand, clattering to the ground with a pathetic thump. It was a disaster. As I shamefully reached down to grab the clipboard, I had to come to terms with that fact that I'll never be as intimidating as Snape. I felt like a failure until I realized that if I walked into a class with a Snape-like attitude, I'd only receive sneers in return. But if I made a subconscious effort to walk in with a positive attitude, my students and I would leave class feeling better.

The paradox of Snape is such: he can keep a class silent, but that doesn't mean students will listen. There is no internal motivation to perform or behave in his class other than fear. In *Chamber of Secrets,* Harry, Ron and Hermione need ingredients for their Polyjuice Potion and decide the only way they could obtain them was from Snape's cupboard. During class, Harry throws a firework into a potion, splashing nearby students whose body parts begin to swell and providing an adequate distraction for Hermione to quietly slip in and steal the ingredients. These are among Snape's most hated students. They are definitely afraid of him. But this doesn't stop them from ruining his lesson. Professor McGonagall is just as strict, but if the ingredients were in her storage instead, I'm sure they would have chosen an alternative to theft and disruption out of respect.

Simply put, students do not respect Snape because he is unfair. He often snaps at them when they're not copying down what he's saying, even when he hasn't instructed them to do so. Most prominently, he favors the Slytherins over all the other houses. In *Prisoner of Azkaban*, Malfoy comes late to Potions and disrupts the entire lesson. If this were anyone else, they would have received detention and multiple rude comments. Snape, however, only tells Malfoy to *"settle down."*[4] He also frequently walks about the room criticizing everyone except Malfoy. Is Draco really that good at Potions? We only see Harry's perspective, and Harry hates him, so it is possible. But even if Malfoy was exceptionally good, this is unacceptable behavior. There's no reason he should pick on other students based on their failures.

Snape takes favoritism way too far. He obviously favors the Slytherins and this turns everyone else against him. For example, in *Goblet of Fire* when Harry and Malfoy begin attacking each other, Snape only listens to Malfoy's side of the story and takes points from the Gryffindors along with assigning them detention. Harry himself feels that the *injustice of it made him want to curse Snape into a thousand pieces.*[5] To make matters worse, Harry, Ron and Hermione now have to sit through a whole class period with Snape and the Slytherins after being treated so unfairly. It would be hard for anyone to learn in that environment, much less fourteen-year-olds who already have enough going on in their personal lives to start with.

Snape often gives Harry low grades, tries to get him kicked off the Quidditch team and takes extra points away from Gryffindor students for the smallest issues like bringing a library book outside. Because that's what we want of course, to encourage students not to read. Favoring the Slytherins alienates three-quarters of the student population and makes learning in his classroom a chore. When students need to decide between listening to Snape or defying him, it will come down to one thing: he doesn't treat his students with respect, and in turn, they don't respect him.

Some of the unfairness in our classrooms happens quite unintentionally. We all have favorites, even if we don't want to. It just happens. Our classes are a diverse mix of athletes, cheerleaders, musicians, troublemakers and much more. One year I had a class with a standard mix, just with a couple of leadership students who were much more talkative than the rest and would come visit me after school. As the year progressed, I slowly allowed them to get away with more and more things. Nothing major. Just simple things like not saying anything if they were eating in my class, something I didn't allow at the time. Or if they moved to sit by their friend. Or if they were talking too much. They were all still completing their work and they had good grades, what did it really matter? But it did matter. I had unintentionally created favorites.

I didn't reflect on how this looked to my other students until I opened my copy of *Sorcerer's Stone* later that summer. I'm sure some of them felt indignant like Harry, Ron and Hermione whenever Professor Snape favored the Slytherins over them. This was a simple fix. I could have changed things in my classroom immediately, but I wasn't aware of it. I need to constantly be mindful of favoring one group of students over others. This is one reason why I like to change my seating chart. If I move students around, different students get to sit closer to me and I end up having more personal conversations with them. Like Professor Sprout, we need to develop relationships with all our students, not just the ones that seek us out.

Even before we have the chance to see Snape in the classroom, we learn that he *"teaches Potions, but he doesn't want to."* Based on this one sentence, I would think he doesn't care if students are successful because he isn't passionate about potion-making. But in his introductory speech on Harry's first day, he says:

> *"I don't expect you will really understand the beauty of the*
> *softly simmering cauldron with its shimmering fumes, the*

delicate power of liquids that creep through the human veins, bewitching the mind, ensnaring the senses... I can teach you how to bottle fame, brew glory, even stopper death — "[6]

No matter how scary Snape is, this speech makes me want to take his class. I picture myself mixing ingredients to perfection, creating a shimmering gold cauldron full of liquid luck or stirring the pearly love potion...and I can barely cook dinner for myself.

In *Half-Blood Prince*, Professor Snape is finally given the chance to teach Defense Against the Dark Arts, the subject he has been longing to teach all these years. Again, his speech the first day shows his passion:

> *"The Dark Arts," said Snape, "are many, varied, ever-changing, and eternal. Fighting them is like fighting a many-headed monster, which, each time a neck is severed, sprouts a head ever fiercer and cleverer than before. You are fighting that which is unfixed, mutating, indestructible."*
>
> *"Your defenses," said Snape, a little louder, "must therefore be as flexible and inventive as the arts you seek to undo."*[7]

Snape is clearly passionate about his subject. Hermione even compares this inspiring speech to the one Harry gave prior to the formation of Dumbledore's Army. If passion isn't stopping him from reaching students, then what is? His first speech in *Sorcerer's Stone* continues with one more line: "*— if you aren't as big a bunch of dunderheads as I usually have to teach.*"[8] Oh. There's the problem. Snape is just as passionate about Potions and Defense Against the Dark Arts as Flitwick is about Charms. There's one huge difference—Flitwick is also passionate about his students' success.

✳ ✳ ✳

All of Professor Snape's lessons are interactive. He essentially runs a lab class. Each day he posts instructions for their potion on the board, then sits menacingly behind his desk. On their first day of class in Harry's fifth year, Snape gives these instructions for mixing a Draught of Peace:

> *"Be warned: If you are too heavy-handed with the ingredients you will put the drinker into a heavy and sometimes irreversible sleep, so you will need to pay close attention to what you are doing.... The ingredients and method"* — *Snape flicked his wand* — *"are on the blackboard"* — *(they appeared there)* — *"you will find everything you need"* — *he flicked his wand again* — *"in the store cupboard"* — *(the door of the said cupboard sprang open)* — *"you have an hour and a half.... Start."* [9]

That's all the instructions he gives them. They are left alone to attempt what sounds like a very complicated potion with the potential to curse one of their classmates with eternal slumber. Yet, he doesn't provide any assistance. The only other instruction he gives comes when the class has 10 minutes left, *"A light silver vapor should now be rising from your potion."*

In contrast to the collaborative and interactive work taking place in Professor Sprout's and Professor Flitwick's classrooms, he does not monitor or encourage students to improve. They are left to fail on their own, until he walks by at the end of the period to judge and insult their work. Hermione's work produces a shimmering silver color like Snape told them it should, but he offers no compliment.

He moves on to Harry's and points out his mistakes in front of the whole class, asking *"Can you read? ... Did you do everything on the third line...?"* When Harry looks back at the board, he realizes he forgot an ingredient and has to shamefully answer 'no.' Snape tells him, *"I know... which means this mess is worthless"* [10] and gives him a zero on the assignment. Perhaps if Snape was monitoring his class and actually cared for them to be successful, he could have reminded Harry to add this ingredient earlier in the class period.

In many ways, Snape is the antithesis of the other Heads of Houses. Sprout, Flitwick and McGonagall are all accepting, conscientious and passionate about helping their students gain knowledge; Professor Snape favors only those from his house, punishes for his own gain, and cares more about his own intelligence rather than the growth of knowledge within his students. If Snape lived up to his potential, perhaps his students would too.

✳ BULLY ✳

After Snape's passionate speech on the first day of lessons, he immediately begins to target Harry. In the movie version of *Sorcerer's Stone*, he initially picks on Harry because Snape thinks he's not paying attention, but Harry had actually been looking down at his paper, writing every word. Snape asks him a question that he knows Harry will never be able to answer, then says, *"Tut, tut — fame clearly isn't everything."* He singles out Harry two more times with nearly impossible questions, each time adding an additional insulting comment. When Harry finally talks back, Snape takes points from Gryffindor. But this isn't Harry's fault, his teacher provoked him. Harry is new to the wizarding world, has just arrived at Hogwarts and is in awe of the place, the magic and the teachers. Then one of the first professors he encounters treats him like scum. It takes only one lesson for Harry to realize that *"Snape didn't dislike Harry — he hated him."*[11]

Snape allows his strong hatred for Harry's father to linger and fuel his abuse. After Harry tries to make a distinction between Inferius and ghosts, Snape wittily replies, *"Yes, it is easy to see that nearly six years of magical education have not been wasted on you, Potter. 'Ghosts are transparent.'"* Snape isn't trying to be funny, he's trying to be malicious and Harry's resentment only grows. Especially when Snape adds *"A five-year-old could have told us as much."*[12] Teachers are often cautioned about using sarcasm in the classroom. When even one person becomes hurt and humiliated by our sarcastic comments, as Snape egregiously demonstrated, then it's not appropriate. I do believe, however, that students have the capacity to understand and appreciate sarcasm.

Professor Snape manages to use sarcasm in *Order of the Phoenix* with more positive effect. When coming across an altercation, he tells Crabbe to loosen his hold, saying, *"If Longbottom suffocates it will mean a lot of tedious paperwork and I am afraid I shall have to mention it on your reference if ever you apply for a job."* [13] I used a similar tactic when I caught one of my sophomore boys lighting a firework and shooting it off into a crowd of students as they were exiting the school. While I still disciplined the Weasley-wannabe, I spun the conversation to be about how inconvenient it was going to be for me now that I had to write him up. It put a new perspective on the situation and when he came back to my class a few days later I was able to repair the relationship and continue to teach him, even though in his eyes I had "turned him in." Often the best use of sarcasm is one where we are the subject of the humor and not the students. Only a personal relationship developed with individual students will help us determine if our sarcasm isn't hurting them. Because Snape is often malicious, he doesn't develop relationships with any of his students, nor does he care if his sarcasm is hurtful or understood.

Most of Professor Snape's vindictiveness is taken out on Harry, but Hermione finds herself on the receiving end of several insults as well. He calls her a *"Stupid girl"* and an *"insufferable know-it-all"* [14]—impressive she's able to pull off both at the same time. He makes fun of the size of her teeth and takes points away when she helps other students in class. It is Neville, however, who I feel most sorry for. Snape's hatred of Harry only fuels him to be more successful in order to prove him wrong, and Hermione is successful no matter the circumstances. Neville, on the other hand, withdraws in Snape's presence and only gets worse at Potions the more time he spends in his class.

On the very first day of lessons, Neville messes up his potion. The stuff spreads everywhere and begins melting people's shoes. As Neville is lying on the ground, embarrassed, covered in boils and in tremendous pain, Professor Snape swoops over, shouts *"Idiot boy!"* [15] and makes sure to point out his mistakes before sending him to the hospital wing.

There are many examples of Snape bullying Neville, but this scene in Prisoner of Azkaban is among the worst:

> *Tell me, boy, does anything penetrate that thick skull of yours? Didn't you hear me say, quite clearly, that only one rat spleen was needed? Didn't I state plainly that a dash of leech juice would suffice?*
>
> …
>
> *"Longbottom, at the end of this lesson we will feed a few drops of this potion to your toad and see what happens. Perhaps that will encourage you to do it properly.*

Hermione helps Neville, so when forced to drink the shrinking potion, Trevor becomes a tadpole. But what would have happened if Hermione hadn't cheated? Would Snape really have let his pet die? Sure, he could revive Trevor, but this is beyond cruel. After this lesson, Neville goes to his next class, only to have Snape bully him again, saying, *"Possibly no one's warned you, Lupin, but this class contains Neville Longbottom. I would advise you not to entrust him with anything difficult."*[16]

Later in the series, Snape assigns Neville detentions when he is failing Potions. Neville isn't choosing to fail Snape's class. Putting him in detention is only going to heighten his fear of his greasy, dark-haired teacher. He needs Professor Snape to be more understanding, compassionate and helpful. Instead, Neville only continues to fail. He becomes so frightened by Snape that when confronted with a boggart, which takes the shape of someone's biggest fear, it doesn't turn into a giant spider, a bandaged mummy, or a bloody eyeball like the other students, it turns into the one person whose job it is to help him feel safe—his teacher.

One year, I was explaining a project where students were required to create their own Cold War Museum. I asked my students how many of them had been to a museum before and about half raised their hands. Then one girl, who often asks questions students saw as dimwitted, raised her hand to ask 'Are aquariums museums?' As usual when she raised her hand, students laughed. Usually she was adept at laughing it off along with them, but this time was different. I laughed as well. As I turned her direction, I saw her smile slowly fade away, the light in her eyes draining. I felt awful. No one noticed except me, but I will never forget that look. I immediately tried to backtrack and explain how aquariums do have exhibits and information organized in a way that is similar to a museum, so that makes perfect sense. But it was too late. I had already made fun of her in front of the class. It hurt her more coming out of my mouth than anything her peers could have said. Professor Snape may be intentionally hostile, but we need to be aware of how we are unintentionally hurting our students.

Fear isn't a new concept in the classroom. Even well-intentioned teachers use fear as a tactic, the threat of unpleasant consequences such as failure or a phone call home always looming. While this may motivate students, it will not in itself create an environment where students are comfortable to learn. Consequences need to be paired with support and kindness for students to truly thrive. McGonagall's conscientious style of disciplining helps change student behavior, whereas Snape's vindictive nature and bullying tendencies only furthers the distance between him and his students. Our classrooms need to be a place where all students feel safe and welcome. We don't want them to feel like Gryffindors walking into the stuffy, Slytherin-favored Potions classroom.

✳ ✳ ✳

Snape is so cruel to Harry in the classroom that even though Snape is trying to protect him, Harry believes he is the one trying to kill him for six whole years. If Snape could find it within himself to be compassionate and caring, he could become a good teacher. As it stands, the only positive thing I can say for sure is that Snape is passionate about his subject. But this passion doesn't transfer to his students and ultimately they don't reach their full potential in his class. This is evident when Snape manages to teach Harry more from his annotated book under the pseudonym Half-Blood Prince than he ever did as his actual Potions professor. Perhaps he would be successful as a teacher in an online school where classes have no face-to-face interaction, but as a Hogwarts professor he is insufficient.

As a fan, I enjoyed Professor Snape's ambiguous personality. For six books I questioned his loyalty and intentions. I thought he was the one attempting to throw Harry off his broom, then realized he was actually saving him. I hated Snape when he tried to give Sirius to the dementors but loved him for protecting his students from the transformed werewolf. And in *Deathly Hallows*, when we learned that Snape—always—loved Harry's mother, I came to truly appreciate the difficult situation he was forced into.

It is this ambiguity, however, that makes him an unsuccessful teacher. Outside of Hogwarts, Snape represents all the traits of the four houses—he is loyal, intelligent, brave and ambitious. But these skills don't transfer to his life inside the school grounds. In the end, he is loyal but only to Dumbledore, loving but only to Lily and protective but only of Harry's physical health and not his emotional well-being. Harry does name his second child after Snape because of his sacrifice, but that doesn't fix the abuse inflicted in his classroom. As a double agent in the wizarding war and a character in the series, Professor Snape will always be remembered as a hero, but as a teacher he only leaves a lasting legacy of hostility.

PROFESSOR SLUGHORN

THEATRICAL * REALIST * VAIN

"As we're so few, we'll do something fun. I want you to brew me up something amusing!" [1]

HEAD OF SLYTHERIN * POTIONS

At the beginning of *Half-Blood Prince*, we meet Professor Slughorn disguised as an armchair. As the Death Eaters gain power, he tries to avoid their influence by moving to a new unoccupied Muggle home every week. When Harry and Dumbledore enter his current residence, they find a living room that looks like it has exploded: cushions are torn apart and blood is splattered across the walls. But Dumbledore isn't fooled by these theatrics and forces Slughorn to transform back from the squashy armchair he had so expertly disguised himself as. Slughorn immediately puts on a cordial tone, acting as if this whole ordeal were an amusing mix-up. Despite this overblown introduction, Harry is not immediately taken to his new teacher.

Professor Slughorn returns to Hogwarts after some convincing and, to

Harry and the other students' surprise, replaces Professor Snape as Potions teacher. Unlike Snape, Slughorn represents all the positive qualities that Slytherins uphold: proud, cunning, and ambitious.

Slytherins get a bad rap throughout the series (with some redemption in Cursed Child), but Slughorn provides us with a great example of the house's redeeming qualities. He chooses to avoid the Death Eaters at all costs, including giving up his comfy life of fame and influence that he loves to display. He does grumble about the apparent death toll of Order of the Phoenix members but ultimately stays on as Head of Slytherin to protect the remaining students and fights alongside the other teachers and students during the Battle of Hogwarts. Professor Slughorn is the best Potions teacher Harry encounters and under his more relaxed teaching style, many of the students finally learn to enjoy the subject.

✳ THEATRICAL ✳

After his peculiar introduction, I was surprised by how well Slughorn handled himself on his first day back at Hogwarts. He thoroughly enjoys being in the spotlight, and this serves him well in the classroom setting.

Slughorn begins class with a few potions laid out as examples of the complex work they will be able to create someday. He chooses three intriguing potions to show them: a cauldron of Veritaserum which makes someone speak the truth, a pearly substance called Amortentia which acts as a strong love potion, and a small cauldron shining with a mysterious golden radiance. Slughorn asks the students for their thoughts and guides them through the process of determining the effect of each potion. Although Hermione commandeers the discussion, this questioning gets the students more involved in the conversation. Slughorn could have easily lectured the class on each of the potion's properties and moved on. Instead, he gets them immediately involved in the process.

As Slughorn elaborates on the nature of love potions, he uses his dramatic character to win them over:

"Amortentia doesn't really create love, of course....It is probably the most dangerous and powerful potion in this room — oh yes," he said, nodding gravely at Malfoy and Nott, both of whom were smirking skeptically.

As I read Slughorn's description of Amortentia, I picture him looking off into the corner of the dreary potions room with clouded vision, as if remembering a crazy time in his past. This would definitely have an effect on students.

In an instant, he acts as if he pulls away from this distant memory and tells them it's time to get to work. But there's still one more cauldron they haven't discussed, which Ernie McMillan excitedly points out:

"Yes. That. Well, that one, ladies and gentlemen is a most curious little potion called Felix Felicis. I take it," he turned, smiling to look at Hermione, who had let out an audible gasp, "that you know what Felix Felicis does, Miss Granger?"

"It's liquid luck," said Hermione excitedly. "It makes you lucky!"

The whole class seemed to sit up a little straighter. [2]

Slughorn didn't forget to introduce the last potion, he simply knows how to utilize omission for dramatic effect. Flitwick earns students' respect through his enthusiasm and McGonagall with her consistency, but Slughorn channels his own dramatic personality to win over students' trust. Their admiration as well, I suppose, knowing his tendency to seek fame and influence. By adding this flair of drama to the classroom he makes his lesson much more interesting. Now he has their undivided attention. This is key. He has won them over.

Adding a little theatricality to any given lesson can help break up the monotony. As an introvert, any mention of the spotlight scares me. People question my career choice all the time once they realize how reserved and quiet I am. Even my students question it when I tell them just how much

I despise being around large groups of people. The difference, however, is that in my classroom I'm in control. It is a space that I have made comfortable. I build relationships with my students and let small parts of my life influence my classroom. To pull this off I put on an amplified version of my own personality. I could never wear a full historical costume or give an entertaining monologue. Instead, I insert my personality with theatrical moments in smaller doses.

One year when I was teaching my eighth grade students about the Intolerable Acts prior to the American Revolutionary War, I sensed there was a barrier preventing them from understanding the way the colonists felt during this time. I tried to explain it to them in a variety of ways:

> "Imagine your parents gave you all the freedom to do what you want." A variety of responses were shouted back without permission.
>
> "I would love that!" "I already do what I want!"
>
> "If you could do whatever you want, whenever you want," I continued, "Imagine that right now. Then… all of a sudden, all your freedoms were taken from you. You had a curfew. No cellphone. You were only allowed to go to school and back. Would you be happy?"

They understood this at a base level but I wanted them to really feel it. That evening, I designed an activity to make them experience what the colonists had to endure. All my students were on a free and reduced meal plan that provided them breakfast and lunch free of charge. For many of them these were the only meals they were given throughout the day. I wrote up a fake letter from our principal detailing the removal of this program and distributed it to my students the following day. I printed it on green paper, included the school's emblem and slogan on the top. It looked as official as I dared make it. I assured my principal I would collect every single copy back and make sure they knew it wasn't true. As class began, I passed out the letters and read to them the following passage:

Dear Parent/ Guardian,

I regret to inform you that with all the construction and improvements coming to the campus, our school is running low on funding.

We actually were going through construction at the time so it was somewhat believable. Plus my playacting was spot on... if I say so myself.

Unfortunately, we can no longer afford to have free breakfasts and lunches available for everyone.

My students began to grumble loudly. It was difficult to get to the rest of the letter. But I was finally able to continue.

Starting Tuesday, September 13, breakfast and lunch will cost $2.50 each. I apologize for this inconvenience, but we must make cuts if we want to keep other school programs.

They were livid. Some were out of their seats. Others crumpled up their letters, which was a bit unfortunate because I needed to use these copies for one more class period. Some shouted out. They were clearly upset. It worked, I had successfully provoked them. I gave them a minute to get it out of their system. It felt like my class was a little out of control and I couldn't help but be bothered by this. I like order and structure in my classes, but I just kept telling myself this was part of the plan. It was hard to keep the smile off my face. I had pulled off an elaborate prank on 30 twelve-year-olds and I'm not going to lie, it was fun.

I eventually told them the truth and had to assure them multiple times that their lunch was still free. After they calmed down, one student said "Ms. D... You got us good. I don't know if I trust you anymore." I laughed and passed out the real assignment as I collected the letters. I reminded them that everything we do in this class is for a purpose. One student yanked the assignment from my hands with a fake dirty look on her face. Then we both laughed as I continued down the row. In the assignment I had the students compare their feelings over the price increase with the colonists' response to the raised prices of stamps, sugar and tea. This extra drama added into the lesson took 5-10 minutes of my class time but now my students understood how the colonists felt way more than through any story I could have told.

Another week I told my students they would be detectives and were hired for a new case. Their job was to determine the real cause of the Roman Empire's collapse. They did research, investigated and proved their findings with evidence. I provided case files that had "Top Secret" and "Classified" written on them. They embraced the activity wholeheartedly and asked me if they could come up with detective and agent names. When I propped the door open to get some fresh air, a student raised her hand and said, "Ms. Dickie, I don't think the door should be open because we have top secret information out and anyone will be able to see it." They had so much fun all while learning how to provide evidence to support their opinion or claim.

In smaller moments when the fate of an empire isn't at stake, I have handed out certificates for games I have created and asked students to come to the front of the class as I put on a small show, shake their hands and pose for a fake camera.

Slughorn understands that small theatrical moments such as these break up the tedium and help keep students focused and interested. When a student asks if Slughorn has ever taken the lucky potion, he responds with:

> *"Twice in my life... Once when I was twenty-four, once when I was fifty-seven. Two tablespoonfuls taken with breakfast. Two perfect days."*
>
> *"And that," said Slughorn, apparently coming back to earth, "is what I shall be offering as a prize this lesson."*[3]

Professor Slughorn is a master of this method. All that's needed is a touch of drama and suddenly Felix Felicis is the enticement that gets the students fully engaged and passionate about Potions within the first day of class. Giving Felix Felicis as a prize is a genius idea. I wish I could hand out liquid luck as a way of rewarding hardworking students, although I am 97.3% positive they would use it for something against the rules. They don't all have Hermiones running around to help be their conscience.

One year I was in a weird contract situation and was moved between schools in the middle of the semester. I was only given two class periods and nothing to fill up the rest of my time. Eventually, due to the rough nature of my school's population, a few teachers quit and I acquired the random elective classes that I could still teach under my credential. These classes became a dumping ground for students who were kicked out of their other classes due to behavioral issues. It was my second year and I had a mix of some of the worst students on campus and was supposed to train them to become peer mediators. Yes, because students who can't manage their own behavior problems would clearly be great at solving other peoples' problems. Even my principal realized there was no way these students would be mediating anyone in a few months and told me I could teach them anything I wanted.

After stressing about what lessons to plan, I decided to teach what was natural to me: Harry Potter. We read through *Sorcerer's Stone* and I created activities to go along with each chapter. We journaled every day, read about historical references mentioned in the book and so much more. At first some complained, but they fell in love with the characters and the story just like many before them. These were students who have gang members for much of their families. Some of them were gang members themselves. And they were sitting there quietly while Jim Dale (the voice of the American Harry Potter audiobooks) and I took turns reading to them.

One day there were two boys in the back who were drawing on each other while I was reading. It was distracting me, but not anyone else so I let it slide. I went to talk to them about it at the end of the class period and as I approached I realized they had drawn lightning bolts on each other's arms. These were students who many would be afraid to approach outside of school and here they were drawing Harry Potter symbols on each other. I had to hold back tears of joy.

Towards the end of the book, I had students work out Snape's riddle themselves. The critical thinking involved in solving a riddle is tremendous. Like Hermione says in *Sorcerer's Stone* "*This isn't magic — it's logic — a puzzle.*"[4] I walked around and provided support when needed. Some would be stuck in there forever, but a good majority figured it out and they were so proud to accomplish a complex task on their own. I gave out two Gryffindor ties to the pair that completed the riddle first. The winners were so excited to earn a prize they could take home with them. When they asked me to tie it for them, I had to admit I didn't know how but directed them to the computer in the corner of the classroom. While the rest of the class finished the riddle themselves, they spent 10 minutes learning how to tie a tie. Not only did this prize reflect what they had been learning in class, they also had the chance to navigate the computer (which was hard for some) and learn a new skill. I love that this prize was so meaningful.

Slughorn's theatrical ability and prize of Felix Felicis had every single students' attention and concentration for the entire class period. That is a beautiful feeling, and for some teachers this comes naturally. I have coworkers who can walk into any room full of students and hold their attention for hours without any tools or plans. It's magical. I really have to work at it. Even my theatrical display of the letter was carefully timed, pre-written and planned out. But I had their attention, and they all learned as well as they would in my coworkers' or Slughorn's classrooms. This will look different for each teacher depending on personality and comfort zone but becoming a bit theatrical in small moments can go a long way.

✳ REALIST ✳

Professor Slughorn is difficult to label. I had trouble pinning down all of the teachers, but Slughorn in particular was hard to understand objectively. We read the stories from Harry's perspective and Harry doesn't particularly like him. Not to mention we witness him giving advice to Voldemort, the details of which Harry spends most of *Half-Blood Prince* trying to figure out. There is something more to his teaching style than we might notice at first. Slughorn exudes a sense of understanding between himself and his students that carefully tiptoes the line of permissive lenience and authoritative criticism. In front of the classroom, his relaxed and pragmatic attitude allows students to work under realistic expectations.

In their first potions lesson, when Slughorn has the students begin preparing a Draught of Living Death he tells them, *"I know it is more complex than anything you have attempted before, and I do not expect a perfect potion from anybody. The person who does best, however, will win little Felix here."*[5] He acknowledges that not all students are going to be able to accomplish tasks at the same rate, something refreshing to hear from a Hogwarts professor especially after dealing with Professor Snape for so long.

At the beginning of the year we are required to complete a planning worksheet called 'SMART' goals. While I absolutely hate filling out this worksheet at the staff meeting, some of it does make sense. If you are unfamiliar, SMART stands for: Specific, Measurable, Achievable, Realistic and Time-Bound. In essence, it challenges you to be able to look back and see that you have accomplished these goals using specific data analysis tools throughout the school year. I'm sure Slughorn would be the teacher that would not only fail to complete the SMART goals sheet at the beginning of the school year but also laugh at anyone using this acronym in real life. In practice, however, he acts out these goals in his classroom better than most. Not all students will accomplish their goals at the same rate. I love that he tells them to not expect perfection. How often do we pressure students to earn a 100% when this is not attainable for most? They automatically feel like failures and this is our fault.

Slughorn's realism helps create a more comfortable atmosphere in the Potions classroom than ever before. In his first class with Slughorn, Harry is finally able to get his potion to turn the perfect pale shade the textbook calls for. Sure, some of this has to be attributed to the Half-Blood Prince a.k.a. Professor Snape himself, but Harry never felt comfortable enough in the first place to thrive in Snape's class. Who knows, maybe Harry could have become excellent at Potions just like his mother with more encouragement and realistic expectations.

Harry also feels comfortable enough to provide the brazen answer of the cure-all bezoar when they are tasked with creating an antidote to an unnamed potion. Slughorn stares at Harry's hand for several seconds before booming, *"You've got nerve, boy!...That's the individual spirit a real potion-maker needs!"* [6]

Professor Slughorn openly accepts Harry's creative and unorthodox answer. It upsets pretty much everyone else in the classroom, even Ron and Hermione, but Slughorn loves it. We need to be able to respond as Slughorn does and reward creativity, even if it undermines our teaching a bit. Still, Harry doesn't learn how to make an antidote for an unknown poison, probably an important skill to have in the wizarding world, so I hope that Slughorn revisits this in a later lesson we are not privileged to see.

I once split students up into class systems according to medieval Japanese society. Feudal Japan's pyramid looks roughly like this— Emperor (figurehead), Shogun (real leader), Daimyo (wealthy landowners), Samurai, Artisans & Merchants, and Peasants. Each student had a specific role they were required to carry out in their groups throughout the class period. At one point the class became fairly rowdy and I yelled "Hey, Emperor... your country is in chaos!" I had assigned him the job of making sure everyone in his group was staying on task. His reply was genius, "Blame it on my Shogun, not me!" I laughed just as much as Slughorn did in response to Harry's display of the bezoar.

Even when responding with, as J.K. Rowling writes, 'cheek,' each of these students demonstrated further understanding of the subject matter. Like Slughorn, we need to be willing to accept and embrace these creative responses. I, for one, don't want to create students who all think alike. I want them to think for themselves and come up with new responses to old questions. We are preparing students more than ever before for jobs that don't currently exist. We need them to be able to think on their toes and come up with new solutions. Our world is changing rapidly and our classrooms need to change with it.

* VAIN *

While Professor Slughorn has some great teaching moments, he does have obvious faults. Albus Dumbledore describes his colleague as someone who:

> *"Likes the company of the famous, the successful and the powerful. He enjoys the feeling that he influences these people....He used to handpick favorites at Hogwarts, sometimes for their ambition or their brains, sometimes for their charm or their talent, and he had an uncanny knack for choosing those who would go on to become outstanding in their various fields."* [7]

Professor Slughorn's desire to be influential causes him to favor students for their potential and ignore those he deems unpromising. These students are related to powerful people, may become famous one day, or in Harry's case, are already famous. He collects them, invites them to join his Slug Club and holds parties every so often to get to know them better. He admits to Harry when they first meet that *"You shouldn't have favorites as a teacher, of course, but she was one of mine. Your mother..."* Slughorn goes on to tell Harry he regrets that Sirius was placed in Gryffindor and not in his house, because he would have *"liked the set."* [8]

Slughorn's favoritism rekindles itself as he returns to Hogwarts in Harry's sixth year as the new Potions teacher. In fact, the preferential treatment begins even before they arrive to Hogwarts. Harry, Neville, Ginny and others are given a note on the Hogwarts express asking them to meet Slughorn in his compartment. Slughorn introduces them all, subtly describing their access to fame and then name drops people who he is personally connected to.

Preferential treatment of this group of students lasts the whole school year. These students get invited to parties where they meet vampires and swap success stories. Slughorn goes out of his way in the corridors to say hello and ask them if they need anything. This sounds exciting for members of the Slug Club, but their professor is essentially using them in hope of gaining favors later in life. Blaise Zabini is singled out for his mother's promiscuity and scandal surrounding her former husbands' deaths. Neville is chosen because his parents were tortured as part of their involvement in the fight against Lord Voldemort. These are personal matters that they have successfully hidden from their classmates. And right now their professor is inviting them to a dinner party and discussing their secrets over a bowl of ice cream. Teenagers are especially vulnerable to this subtle manipulation by their mentors. Slughorn isn't thinking of his students, he only wants to further his influence even if they get hurt in the process.

But at least members of the Slug Club get invited to meet famous people. Those who are not on this list of influential students, however, often get overlooked. Ron never gets invited to any of the parties and this begins to irritate him. On top of that, Slughorn completely ignores him on several occasions outside the classroom, even referring to him as Rupert—a fun nod to the actor, but not great for Ron Weasley himself. We know from the first moment Harry meets Ron that he is self-conscious of being less talented than those around him. In the Mirror of Erised, Ron sees himself as Head Boy, Quidditch Captain and holding the House Cup.

He is jealous of Harry's fame and when Slughorn ignores him outside of the classroom he can't help but feel inferior. Students are more aware of what their teachers think of them than we might think, and even small gestures can have a huge impact on them. Like the previous Potions master, Professor Snape, Slughorn's favoritism negatively affects his students.

Unlike Snape, however, Slughorn's favoritism doesn't necessarily get in the way of his teaching ability. He gives grades out fairly, makes sure to monitor all students' progress and gives everyone helpful comments. While in the classroom he teaches everyone the same, but outside it is a completely different story. Ron and other students like him would have learned better if they felt their professor actually remembered their names and cared about them outside of obligation.

* * *

While Slughorn excels in many ways inside the classroom, he is still flawed. And let's remember that his only other comparison when it comes to a Potions teacher is Professor Snape, someone who loathes Harry's existence. He gets drunk with Hagrid in Harry's presence following Aragog's funeral. He constantly ignores students who he deems as less important than others outside the classroom. He is known to toot his own horn quite often. And he is not quick to defend Muggle-borns, something that turns Harry off to him immediately. Not to mention, he inadvertently encourages the darkest wizard of all time to split his soul into seven pieces. He has his flaws, but we all do, and his redeeming qualities propel him to be one of Harry's better professors.

Professor Slughorn, like the other Heads of Houses, represents traits outside of his own house. He is brave enough to stay on while Voldemort controls Hogwarts, smart enough to understand complex potion-making and although he does have favorites, tries to be accepting of all students. Sure, McGonagall, Flitwick, and Sprout embody these traits wholeheartedly while Slughorn somewhat begrudgingly takes on the role. But as a flawed person, I am encouraged by Slughorn's imperfections knowing it's possible to have issues and still be a great teacher. I have never done anything as bad as encourage a wizard to kill for immortality, but I admire his ability to move past the bad moments and grow as an educator. I hope I can do the same. In a way, coming back to Hogwarts was probably therapeutic for Slughorn. He was able to reconcile with Harry and Dumbledore and even redeem himself as he fought alongside the Order of the Phoenix in the fight against his former student, Lord Voldemort. And he does all this while educating young students about the importance of potions, anecdotes and networking.

PART II: ELECTIVES AND THEIR EMERGENCY REPLACEMENTS

HAGRID

*

PROFESSOR GRUBBLY-PLANK

*

PROFESSOR TRELAWNEY

*

FIRENZE

HAGRID

INSECURE * INCOGNIZANT

"Hasn' — hasn' anyone bin able ter open their books?" said Hagrid,
looking crestfallen.
"I — I thought they were funny."[1]

CARE OF MAGICAL CREATURES

Rubeus Hagrid is the scruffy half-giant groundskeeper at Hogwarts. As a student he was expelled for harboring a huge spider who took the blame for the murder of a student. In reality it was Lord Voldemort's loyal monstrosity, but it's pretty bad when there's only slight differences between the darkest wizard's pet and your own.

Hagrid's love of dangerous creatures continues throughout the entire series. He sends twelve-year-olds into the Forbidden Forest at night, has students take care of beasts that shoot fire out their bums and asks Harry, Ron and Hermione to teach a handsy giant conversational English. By all appearances, he could have been the series' biggest villain. Instead, he is one of the most loving people in Harry's life and his first real friend.

Dumbledore recognizes Hagrid's true character and allows him to become part of the Hogwarts staff first as gamekeeper and later as Care of Magical Creatures professor. His love of magical beasts and his favorite students, however, isn't enough to make him successful in the classroom. It is his inadequacies and insecurity that ultimately result in miseducation and revulsion of the subject he is so passionate about.

✳ INSECURE ✳

Hagrid is more than knowledgeable of his subject matter and has an enthusiasm for magical beasts that would rival Dobby's love of socks. Anyone familiar with Hagrid knows he'd be thrilled to share this passion with students. Although he has the potential for a successful class, Hagrid's insecurities quickly get in the way of magical teaching.

When introducing himself to Harry in *Sorcerer's Stone*, Hagrid tells him, *"Call me Hagrid…everyone does."*[2] By allowing Harry to refer to him simply by his surname he places himself in a position that demands less respect. Harry needs a friend at this point in his life, but more importantly he needs a mentor.

While I was still in college, I took my first coaching position at my alma mater under my former coach. He and the players would refer to me by my first name. I wasn't bothered at the time, I still felt I had the players' respect. The following year, however, I began to student teach at this same school. I had to tell my players that when we were on campus it was no longer appropriate for them to address me by my first name. Understandably, it was hard for them to break this habit. I had always been Dani to them. Even so, I cringed internally every time I saw a player on campus that year, sometimes changing my route to avoid the possibility of another student witnessing this awkward first name interaction. I had set myself up for failure. How could I expect other students to respect me when they see my players talk to me as they would their peers? I was the only one to blame. I should have set the precedent early on that they were to call me coach.

Although Hagrid and I were simply carrying on a habit from before we became teachers, this created lasting problems for us both. When Hagrid is compared to the rest of the staff who are referred to as professor and mister or madam, it is noticeable. Even Mrs. Norris has a title in front of her name and she's a cat! When Harry refers to Professor Snape simply as 'Snape,' it is seen as a blatant sign of disrespect. Other professors are constantly correcting this behavior, including Hagrid himself. Imagine if students were asked to call him Mr. Hagrid. When I hear that name I picture a comically formal version of Hagrid in his best suit and a top hat. And yet, it sounds so odd. It's wrong. He's Hagrid, just Hagrid. As readers, we don't place Hagrid on the same level as the other teachers. The fact that Mr. Hagrid or Professor Hagrid sounds weird says a lot about his status with the students.

As someone who has grown up with an easily made fun of last name, I am aware of the power of names. I remember my dad sitting me down to have a serious discussion about the meaning of our last name and why some kids would find it funny. As a six-year-old, this was lost on me. But my parents were concerned enough to consider changing my name on school records before entering kindergarten. As I grew, the torment was never at the level my brothers received, but I still got the occasional "Dani Sucky Dickie" or the suggestion that I change my name to Harry (it had nothing to do with my love of Harry Potter). Kids are so clever.

After learning from my previous mistakes, I try to make it clear from day one what I want my students to call me. I tell them, "I know my name can be awkward, so let's address it right now. I have had this name my entire life. If you think you can come up with something I haven't heard already, you will not. Trust me." I pause for effect, as I'm sure some of them are quietly trying to devise some creative amendment to my name. They have yet to prove me wrong. I continue, "So if saying Dickie makes you uncomfortable, that's fine, just call me Ms. D. I'll answer to that as well. Can we move past this now?" A few students always smile awkwardly and nod their head. Addressing this potentially awkward moment gives me the authority, my name is my own and I decide how I will be thought of.

As Hagrid takes on a teaching role his name is the least of his worries. We get a sense that he doubts his ability as a professor before the first lesson even begins. On the first day of class, he leads his students over to a fenced-in area and tells them to open their books. Draco asks, rather rudely, *"How?³"* Hagrid is taken aback. It takes only one word for him to begin doubting himself.

Teaching is a profession full of decisions. We have to make big decisions and small, split-second decisions all day long. One of the first choices Hagrid made after he decided to accept Dumbledore's appointment as Care of Magical Creatures professor was to choose a textbook. I imagine Hagrid pouring over books about magical creatures. He probably owns some of his own. Maybe he went to the Hogwarts library to peruse their collection. I bet he skimmed through them all, finally deciding on *The Monster Book of Monsters*. Maybe it was informational, had great pictures, and covered all the creatures he wanted to introduce to his classes. I'm sure he imagined Harry, Ron and Hermione's reactions to the book, his three favorite students at Hogwarts. He pictured the delight on Hermione's face when she saw the content and the humor in Ron's when the book tried to bite him. This small interaction with Draco shatters Hagrid's image of how his first lesson would go. With one simple question, he stops believing in himself.

Hagrid somewhat recaptures the students' attention and his own confidence upon their first glimpse of hippogriffs. The students are amazed by the beauty of such an interesting and unique creature. He begins to tell students some important information, *"Easily offended, hippogriffs are. Don't never insult one, 'cause it might be the last thing yeh do."* But the Slytherins are not listening and Hagrid makes the mistake of continuing to talk without first gaining their attention.

Hagrid is trying to give a lesson that would help students fall in love with magical creatures, and by all means this lesson could have been amazing for those listening. However, he lets them all down when he doesn't make the Slytherins stop to listen. This is a dangerous first lesson to introduce to his lowest level class, the least he could do is make sure all precautions are in order. So when Malfoy gets a turn with Buckbeak, he calls him a *"great ugly brute"*[4] and is greeted with sharp talons. Most of the students blame the injury on Draco, the trio among the loudest. He wasn't listening and if he had been he would have known not to insult the hippogriff. But Hagrid is still the adult in this situation. If there is any problem, the blame falls on the teacher. We have to try to maintain awareness in our classes at all times.

To ensure more success, Hagrid should have stopped in the middle of his speech, addressed Malfoy, Crabbe and Goyle and made them quiet down. And having one hippogriff out instead of several would make it easier to monitor students individually as they were bowing and working with the new creature. He smartly has Harry demonstrate what to do, but then too quickly allows the rest of the class to split up and work with the hippogriffs on their own. This means his attention is divided and when a problem arises he is not able to fix it quickly.

Sure, a student being attacked by a large creature isn't a great start to his teaching career, but these moments are temporary. His biggest mistake is letting these events get to his head. As Harry, Ron and Hermione walk down to Hagrid's hut later to check on him, they find him drunk and crying, convinced he is going to be fired.

The stress of the first year of teaching is immense. Many teachers quit within the first five years when not given adequate support, even when they have the same level of passion as Hagrid. I understand the desire to quit. I had many such moments in my first year of teaching where the students were behaving terribly or my lessons were complete failures.

There were many days where I wanted to cry. But I made sure that I never did this in front of my students. Sometimes I had to close and lock the door between periods and mentally compose myself before facing the next group of students. I learned early on that I would never survive as a teacher if I didn't let myself be encouraged by the small victories.

As I was teaching a lesson on the Civil War and trying to help students understand the meaning of the word secession, I asked a student to quiet down and he became upset. He got out of his seat and shouted "I want to secede from this class!" He looked ready to accept my anger, almost bracing himself for what would come next. The day before I had sent him out for a similar outburst, but this time I decided to take a new approach. I looked at him and said, "Jason, I taught you something today!" I was so excited that he had mastered the meaning of secession that I couldn't keep the smile off my face. He was so shocked by my response that he sat down and continued to take notes. While not much, this little moment helped carry me through the rest of the day. As a teacher, there are so many tough incidents that we end up dwelling on. Hagrid needs to remember the times that make him smile and remind him why he's proud to be a teacher. Instead, he becomes overwhelmed with his deficiencies and lets this affect his ability to teach.

Unfortunately, Hagrid's insecurities and moments of weakness don't improve much by the end of this same school year. When Buckbeak is sentenced to death he cries in front of Harry, Ron and Hermione and the trio are forced to calm him down. He even tells them that he can't afford to fall apart and tries to give himself a mini pep talk. Regardless, he still dwells on the situation when he's needed as a teacher. During a lesson he pulls the three of them aside to discuss the verdict. After failing to keep his composure, he ends up running back to his cabin, trying to hide his tear-soaked face. Malfoy, Crabbe, and Goyle, who already didn't consider Hagrid an authority figure, lose any shred of respect they still had for him. Malfoy even goes as far as exclaiming, *"Have you ever seen anything quite as pathetic?...And he's supposed to be our teacher!"*[5]

Hagrid has a legitimate reason to be upset. And while I know all too well that it's difficult to prevent moments like this from affecting our teaching, he lets it happen too frequently. It's hard not to carry personal matters over to our class time. I want to be real with my students and share my life with them, but at the same time they are there to learn and my bad days should never take that away from them.

One year, a friend of mine was pregnant with her third child. She found out pretty early on that her baby had a syndrome that is nearly always fatal. I got the text on Saturday night at 7:57 p.m. that Darcy was born. The doctors gave her 48 hours to live. On Tuesday night I had more news that she had a steady heartbeat and was eating. My friend and her family were feeling more positive, there was even an adorable picture sent with the text. She was asleep with a slight smile on her face and her hand curved up by her chin. They had been praying for a miracle and this looked like the beginning of one.

I received a text on my lunch break the next day informing me she had passed. I was heartbroken for my friend and her family. We were all so optimistic the night before and in a moment all of that was wrenched from them. It was painful, but I had to teach again in 25 minutes. As I read the text, I was surrounded by a group of teachers and I began to tear up. A friend of mine asked if I was okay and I lied. I knew that if I spoke it aloud I wouldn't be able to hold my emotions in. It would mean admitting this was real. This was final.

I left the lunch room early that day, opened my classroom door and tried to focus on my work. It was hard. My students could tell from the start that something was wrong. I wasn't my normal self. I decided to tell them my friend lost her baby and they sympathized, but I still had a lesson to do and tried to move on. It wasn't my best day of teaching, but I managed to make it through the last period before I turned into a blubbering idiot.

Hagrid and I had every right to cry. Emotion itself is not the problem. However, emotion constantly getting in the way of our teaching abilities can be a serious issue. There is a time and a place for injecting our lives and motivations into our classrooms, but we can't let our personal problems completely affect the learning process.

✳ ✳ ✳

Hagrid's insecurities lead him to seek approval from those around him, often causing him to reach out to Harry, Ron and Hermione for their opinions. He wants them to like him and to be their friend. This is a hard line to cross for teachers. I have had students abruptly ask me if we are friends. Each time I play it off lightly, saying "No, I'm your teacher, everyone knows teachers and students can't be friends," but I can tell that some of them are hurt by this. I know some teachers that let their students come to them with their personal problems and even spend time with them outside of school. While I'm sure the students love this, we have to be careful not to overstep our boundaries. It's far too easy to get in trouble for these kinds of actions. Understandably so, the safety of our students takes priority.

Before becoming students of his, Harry, Ron and Hermione considered Hagrid a close friend and they continue to carry this role even when he becomes their teacher. Hagrid often turns to them for approval of his lessons. The three of them feel obligated to help Hagrid feel better, putting them in an awkward position where they're forced to lie to their professor:

> "I've not bin meself lately,... Worried abou' Buckbeak, an' no one likin' me classes—"
> "We do like them!" lied Hermione at once.
> "Yeah, they're great!" said Ron, crossing his fingers under the table. [6]

I once had a student say to me: "You know, Ms. Dickie. We figured something out about you at lunch today. We realized there are three types of teachers. The first type, tries to be cool and be interested in what we like. They pretend they are young and come off all fake. The second type of teacher is just naturally cool and all the students like them. They don't have to pretend to like what we like because they already do. Then there's you—"

I'm a little confused at this point because so far I would rather be this second type of teacher. I don't want to try really hard to get students to like me, but I would be lying if I didn't want them to like me at all. Who doesn't want to be considered naturally cool?

She continued, "You don't care what students think about you. Or if you are into the stuff we like. You are just concerned with teaching us and making sure we understand history."

At first I was a little hurt by this comment. I was transported back to my high school years for a few minutes. Am I not cool? Do the other kids not like me? Then, as the lesson progressed and I finally shook these stupid doubts out of my head I realized that in Aubree's weird roundabout way she was complimenting me. She was telling me that she appreciated that I didn't pretend to be someone else. I wasn't trying to be their friend, but instead focused my time and energies on teaching them.

In Aubree's words, Hagrid is the first type of teacher. He wants the students to like him so much that he becomes consumed with this one aspect of teaching. Maybe if he had a student as blunt as Aubree then she could have told him to get over it and do his job.

Hagrid's insecurities stem from allowing too many people to have an effect on him. Sure, he has the added pressure of Malfoy trying his hardest to get him fired, Rita Skeeter publishing defamatory articles about him and Umbridge's rude observations to deal with. But in trying to address all criticism, he ends up disappointing everyone, most of all himself.

Instead of moving past the negative reviews, he allows it to affect his teaching. He changes his lessons from exciting beasts like hippogriffs to the least interesting creatures in the wizarding world—flobberworms. As the end of the semester approaches, the stress of the year even causes him to create a test where students simply had to keep their flobberworms alive. Since they thrived best when left alone, students just had to sit around for an hour in order to pass the exam. Clearly, as Harry points out, *his heart didn't seem to be in it at all.*[7] These moments only manage to make Hagrid feel worse about himself, continuing the cycle of doubt.

Hagrid does have some brilliant teaching moments, however, that I don't want to overlook. After an abysmal first semester, Hagrid starts off the next semester strong by having students observe salamanders within a bonfire. He seems refreshed and ready to attempt creative lessons again. And in *Goblet of Fire*, after taking a break from teaching, he resumes his classes and continues with Grubbly-Plank's work on unicorns then moves to nifflers, creatures that seek out treasure. During these lessons, students actually enjoy themselves under Hagrid's instruction and are never afraid of serious injury.

While in the credential program, one of my required readings was Stephen Covey's *7 Habits of Highly Effective People.*[8] My professor felt habit number seven, titled Sharpen the Saw, was the most important for teachers. Covey explains that leaders are very busy people and spend most of their waking moments working or helping others. Therefore, they need to set aside time for personal activities that help re-energize and renew. The theory being, if you take time to sharpen a saw, it will cut through wood all the better. In a leadership capacity, activities that benefit our health, whether physical or mental, will help breathe new life into our work.

That year in the credential program, I learned just how busy life can get for a teacher. I spent all day in the classroom, all night in class at the University, all weekend working on lesson plans and homework, and any extra hours at work trying to make any amount of money I could. I have never felt that overwhelmed or that pushed in my entire life. I loved and hated every moment. Every Monday our professor would ask us to share what we did to sharpen our saw over the weekend. At first I felt it was an unnecessary exercise, especially since I didn't like sharing personal information with the class. I usually made up a random activity or copied the person before me in order to receive credit for the assignment.

Then one weekend I went to see Harry Potter and the Chamber of Secrets live in concert. The next week I went in for an early morning meeting and still had the music in my mind. My friend noticed my cheesy grin and said, "You're awfully cheery for a Monday. Did you do something fun this weekend?" I didn't think much of this comment until a student later told me, "You're in a good mood... You haven't been yourself the past week." This was the first weekend in a while that I had put aside time for myself. I hadn't realized how stressed and overwhelmed I was feeling until some of that weight was lifted. While Covey probably didn't have Harry Potter concerts in mind when he wrote about ways leaders can re-energize, it helped me understand the importance of taking time for myself. It was a benefit not only for me, but for my students as well.

I imagine Hagrid took some time over the holidays to do activities he enjoyed outside of work. He hung out with Fang, his oversized boarhound, or maybe he spent time with Harry, Ron and Hermione trying to find a way to win Buckbeak's case. He finally was able to sharpen his saw. For a moment, he pushed his insecurities aside, and his lessons and students benefited from his improved mental health. Hagrid has moments of brilliance where the lesson runs smoothly and students are interested, but whenever his confidence slips, he falls back on mundane lessons that even Harry, Ron and Hermione come to loathe.

* INCOGNIZANT *

Hagrid doesn't let his students down just because of his insecurities. Many students dread the arrival of his lessons because he fails to know what is going on around him, doesn't learn from his mistakes and isn't aware of the dangers he puts his students in.

The first instance readers see of Hagrid putting kids in danger is in Harry's first year, prior to becoming a professor. At the time, Hagrid is put in charge of Harry, Hermione, Neville and Draco for detention. Hagrid isn't to blame for sending students into the Forbidden Forest at night, but he is the one tasked with overseeing the detention. His first big mistake is pairing Neville with Malfoy and then sending them off into the forest alone with only Fang, his pet dog, to guard them. Seriously? They are eleven. Not to mention, Hagrid did an awful job pairing these two together. Anybody can figure out that Malfoy is the school bully and Neville is the frequent victim. They have already had a number of run-ins this year and now he is sending them into a forest at night without any supervision. When Malfoy gets the opportunity, he grabs Neville while he's not looking in an attempt to scare him. Hagrid needs to be aware of these types of relationships and take precautions to protect Neville from this unnecessary harm.

In *Chamber of Secrets*, Hagrid sends Harry and Ron into the Forbidden Forest again. This time with instructions to follow the spiders. They are led into a den of acromantulas that want to kill them. They do find out that Hagrid is innocent but not before thousands of giant spiders try to rip their heads off. Hagrid puts way too much faith in Aragog and puts the boys in far more risk than he could have easily anticipated. Even after all that, Hagrid asks Harry, Ron and Hermione to enter the forest a third time to help keep Grawp, his giant half-brother, company. I once had a guy invite me to go hiking in the mountains as our first date. It was two hours from the city and there wouldn't have been any cell service. He kept on insisting he would bring snacks, like that would make me feel better about meandering through the woods with a stranger. What was he thinking?? Just because he and Hagrid both felt safe doesn't mean everyone feels the same.

In *Goblet of Fire*, Hagrid introduces his students to Blast-Ended Skrewts, slimy exploding shell-less lobsters who have legs sticking out every direction. The students are disgusted by this new creature and immediately question the purpose of his lesson. Hagrid thinks hard for a few seconds yet can't come up with an adequate reply. If their own professor can't come up with a reason why they should study Blast-Ended Skrewts then why should the students care? After several lessons with the Skrewts, students are burned and dragged and eventually spend their class-time hiding in Hagrid's hut just to avoid the foul creatures. One lesson, as students are attempting to combat these revolting beasts, Hagrid asks Harry if it looks like they're having fun. His classmates were in obvious pain, so Harry assumes Hagrid is talking about the Skrewts. But what if Hagrid was actually referring to his students? So far he has demonstrated a complete lack of awareness to the dangers he puts them in. Perhaps he thinks this lesson is beneficial? No matter his thought processes, Hagrid needs to be more aware of the dangers in his classroom as well as the unimportance of studying creatures that will have no lasting impact on his students' lives outside of Hogwarts. Sure, Care of Magical Creatures is a dangerous subject. Professor Kettleburn, the teacher prior to Hagrid, retired in order to spend more time with his remaining limbs. But all the classes at Hogwarts have the potential to be dangerous—it is a school of magic after all—so Hagrid needs to be just as conscientious as the rest of the professors.

During the next year, Hagrid introduces his students to thestrals, creatures only visible to those who have seen death. The students are rightfully nervous and begin to question Hagrid on the safety of these new beasts. Instead of providing reassurance, he tells them—while his face is scraped and bruised—to stop asking stupid questions and follow him into the forest. His injuries are the result of interactions with his half-brother, not the thestrals, but his students have no way of knowing this. All they know is their professor is injured and leading them into the Forbidden Forest for another lesson with mysterious and potentially dangerous creatures. Hagrid needs to see that his students are apprehensive and do a better job reassuring them and preparing them for the task at hand. They interact with thestrals at least once a year as they take the ride from Hogsmeade up to the castle prior to the start of term. Telling them this would have been a great introduction to the creatures, not only connecting them to the students' lives but giving them a reason to be reassured they won't be harmed. It is important students get a sense of what they're getting into before starting a lesson but Hagrid does little to make his students feel safe while in his care.

Over the course of the series Hagrid continues with the same failed lessons week after week making students dread Care of Magical Creatures. For all his passion of magical beasts, Hagrid fails to recognize his most basic shortcoming as a teacher: his students aren't learning.

✳ ✳ ✳

As I began to bookmark all Hagrid's teaching moments throughout the series I was amazed by the number of times we read about him interacting with students in a teaching capacity. My first thought of Hagrid is never as a teacher, but we actually spend more time reading about him in front of the classroom in three books than most of the professors get in seven. Everyone loves Hagrid as a person. He is a warm, loving character. He spends time putting a photo album together for Harry full of pictures of his parents, supports Ron while he is spewing slug guts and comforts Hermione when she's called foul names. I have no doubt he would do anything to protect these three. During his first three years as a professor, however, he isn't memorable. Even Harry, Ron and Hermione come to dislike his lessons.

Hagrid makes all the mistakes that I did as a first year teacher, but he fails to learn from them. Perhaps this is because of his lack of schooling—

he was expelled during his third year after all. But even with these flaws, he has the potential to become a spectacular teacher. A few deliberate changes would have made all the difference. Hagrid needs someone who can walk alongside and advise him. We don't see any teacher mentoring at Hogwarts, understandable given that teaching is hardly the focus of these novels, but imagine how great Hagrid could have become if someone like Professor McGonagall observed his class and gave him tips. With some assistance, Hagrid could have become more confident in himself and aware of the learning occurring in his classroom. Unfortunately, while Harry, Ron and Hermione are his students, he is never given the opportunity to grow as a teacher and only looks worse in comparison to the substitute teacher that takes over.

PROFESSOR GRUBBLY-PLANK

COMPETENT

"Everyone here? ... Let's crack on then — who can tell me what these things are called?" [1]

CARE OF MAGICAL CREATURES – SUBSTITUTE

As a substitute teacher, some would argue that Professor Grubbly-Plank doesn't belong in this book amongst the full-time staff at Hogwarts. But substitute teachers all around the world are educating our students every day. Grubbly-Plank covers for Hagrid in *Goblet of Fire* when he goes into hiding after Rita Skeeter publishes an article telling the world that he is a half-giant. And in *Order of the Phoenix* she again covers Hagrid's classes when he is away on business for the Order. How do you become a substitute teacher at Hogwarts? Do you have to pass any tests? O.W.Ls? N.E.W.Ts? And why haven't we seen more substitute teachers? The only other teacher to get sick and need a sub day is Professor Lupin in *Prisoner of Azkaban,* and it's Professor Snape who covers for him. Can magic keep away common illnesses? Madam Pomfrey probably deserves more credit.

All substitute teachers have the difficult task of covering classes full of unwelcoming students and teaching unfamiliar lessons. Many are unsuccessful. When Professor Grubbly-Plank takes over as Care of Magical Creatures teacher, however, she immediately makes an impact on the students. She is an accomplished, intelligent professor and the students manage to learn a great deal from her in a short amount of time.

✳ COMPETENT ✳

In many ways Professor Grubbly-Plank does a better job teaching Care of Magical Creatures than Hagrid. Numerous students describe her lessons as more informational and exciting, including highly intelligent characters such as Luna and Hermione. Even Harry begrudgingly recognizes her talents in *Order of the Phoenix*, despite wishing failure on Grubbly-Plank so Hagrid looks better in comparison:

> *"And don't say that Grubbly-Plank woman's a better teacher!…Because she'll never be as good as Hagrid," said Harry firmly, fully aware that he had just experienced an exemplary Care of Magical Creatures lesson and was thoroughly annoyed about it.* [2]

Obtaining highly skilled substitute teachers in the Muggle world is usually much harder than this. I have worked with a few substitutes that were, well, less than competent. Grubbly-Plank on the other hand is quite knowledgeable in the subject and appears to manage a classroom with ease. Did she teach at Hogwarts before? Little is known about her, but from what we do see she clearly has experience.

When I was in high school we had a substitute teacher who everyone remembers as the bagpipe sub. He was super old. Well, now that I think about it he might not have been that old, it could have just been my distorted teenage perception. He would always bring his bagpipes with him and provide a lengthy demonstration. Most students loved it because we couldn't possibly be expected to work while he was playing the bagpipes, right? Now, from a teacher's perspective, I wouldn't be too happy if a substitute teacher had taken up half the class period playing Scottish music. Not to mention, those things are loud. There had to have been some complaints from neighboring teachers.

Unlike the bagpipe substitute, Grubbly-Plank comes in and immediately has students working. The first time she covers for Hagrid she manages to find a unicorn and prepares a full lesson for them at a moment's notice. Afterwards Hermione exclaims, *"That was a really good lesson... I didn't know half the things Professor Grubbly-Plank told us about uni—"*[3] before Harry cuts her off. It's a clear indication of Grubbly-Plank's skills that it only takes one lesson to convince Hermione that she is a capable teacher.

It took me five years of teaching before I discovered a substitute like Grubbly-Plank that I could truly trust. It seems so simple, but I love coming back to my papers organized on my desk, chairs stacked the way I want them and a note explaining the day's events. On other days with other unmentionable subs, I swear Cornish Pixies had been set loose.

In Harry's fifth year Professor Grubbly-Plank returns to Hogwarts and teaches a great lesson on bowtruckles, proving once again that her content knowledge is exemplary. On this day, students walk to Care of Magical Creatures and spot her standing in front of a table with many twigs laying on top. She begins by asking the students to identify the creatures before them. Hermione immediately raises her hand while Parvati and Lavender make noises of excitement. Grubbly-Plank reminds the class to remain quiet and then calls on Hermione to answer the question.

> *"Good girl, take another five points. So whenever you need leaves or wood from a tree in which a bow truckle lodges, it is*

*wise to have a gift of wood lice ready to distract or placate it.
They may not look dangerous, but if angered they will gouge
out human eyes with their fingers, which, as you can see, are
very sharp and not at all desirable near the eyeballs. So if you'd
like to gather closer, take a few wood lice and a bow truckle —
I have enough here for one between three — you can study
them more closely. I want a sketch from each of you with all
body parts labeled by the end of the lesson.* [4]

At this point Professor Grubbly-Plank has covered Hagrid's class the year before and has gotten to know some of the students. It has been a year since she has seen them, yet she picks up where she left off as if no time has elapsed. She addresses each student by name and compliments them when completing tasks or answering questions.

Professor Grubbly-Plank has the ability to handle magical beasts as well as a class of students, a task Hagrid often can't manage. She also handles herself with professionalism, fulfilling all of Hagrid's roles without issue. In contrast, the Muggle world has supplied me with some terrible substitute teachers over the years. Granted, the school I worked at was rough, but they were still unnecessarily invasive while I was away.

One such substitute rifled through my cabinet and proceeded to stick her hands in my Costco-size box of peanut butter pretzels. My students tried to tell her this would upset me but she ignored them, stuck her feet on my desk and continued to chomp away. Seriously? Who does that? She's not Peeves.

Professor Grubbly-Plank would never steal Hagrid's peanut butter pretzels. Yes, his rock cakes are inedible, but this isn't the reason she never rifles through his cabinets to find food. I'm sure she has access to Hagrid's hut as well as all his tools necessary for working with the magical beasts, yet there is never a complaint of her overstepping her boundaries and making other teachers feel uncomfortable. Instead she performs her duties admirably and is an exceptional, if temporary, addition to the teaching staff.

In my second year of teaching there was a male substitute teacher that would frequently cover classes on our campus. He was in his late twenties and a bit on the stocky side. All the girls in my class thought he was gorgeous and wanted me to date him. I just laughed it off and moved on to our lesson.

The students, however, brought up the same conversation with him later that day when they were in their science class. The professional thing to do would be to politely steer the conversation away from the topic. But no—he escalated it. He told them that not only was he going to date me, he was going to marry me. He then allowed the students to take pictures of him flexing his biceps. They ran into my class later that day, told me the news and showed me the pictures. I was outraged. My students couldn't focus for the rest of the day and kept asking me 'Ms. Dickie are you going to marry Gaston?' That's obviously not his actual name, but it should have been! He ruined my classes. And each day he was on campus it would start all over again.

He could have easily avoided the situation, but he played right into their hands. The kids thought it was hilarious and loved every second of it. But they learned nothing that day in both of our classes because of his actions. I understand that substitute teachers are walking into a rough situation, but it would have been very easy for him to simply ignore the question about romantic chemistry and move on to actual chemistry.

On Professor Grubbly-Plank's first day covering Care of Magical Creatures, Harry asks her repeatedly where Hagrid is. Unlike Gaston she does a tremendous job at ignoring Harry's question, staying loyal to Hagrid and continuing to teach the class.

> "Never you mind," she said as though she thought he was being nosy.
>
> "I do mind, though," said Harry hotly. "What's up with him?"

Professor Grubbly-Plank acted as though she couldn't hear him. [5]

The whole wizarding world just found out that a professor at Hogwarts is half-giant. This is huge news. Hagrid is ashamed to show his face even to his own students. I imagine him crying huge, loud ugly tears in his hut all by himself. Harry is legitimately concerned about Hagrid's well-being; Hagrid is his friend and a father figure. Grubbly-Plank, however, doesn't know this. All she knows is that bad news has leaked about their professor and she is here to cover his classes. She could have easily succumbed to the students' pressure. She could have made fun of Hagrid. In fact, she could have effortlessly taken his job if she really wanted. But she does not. She quickly moves on and even compliments Hagrid on his work with thestrals, showing true professionalism and loyalty. This is what we need from our teachers, substitute or otherwise.

Professor Grubbly-Plank finds herself covering for a teacher who is loved around Hogwarts. He may not be the most competent teacher, but the students and staff love Hagrid's hardworking and lovable personality. Grubbly-Plank has a tough role to fill. Those who love Hagrid want her to fail and those who loathe Hagrid don't care to listen to begin with. Like Muggle substitutes, this isn't an easy position to be in. However, she handles every situation with authority and grace. She is knowledgeable enough about the subject matter to plan and organize lessons that are not only relevant to their educational experience but also ones where the students feel safe. And she does all this while handling the class as well as an accomplished professor. Even Harry seeks her out in *Order of the Phoenix* at a time in his life when his trust lies with few people, enlisting her help in healing Hedwig. For someone like Harry to come to trust her within a few class sessions speaks to the admirable job Grubbly-Plank has done as a substitute teacher. I would gladly hire Professor Grubbly-Plank to cover my classes any day, just send me her sub number.

PROFESSOR TRELAWNEY

MELODRAMATIC * INADEQUATE

A voice came suddenly out of the shadows, a soft, misty sort of voice.
"Welcome," it said. "How nice to see you in the physical world at
last." [1]

DIVINATION

Divination is unlike any other class that Harry, Ron and Hermione take. They first meet Professor Trelawney when they begin Divination as an almost randomly chosen new course in their third year at Hogwarts. They enter the Divination classroom after climbing an unfamiliar tower by way of a drop down ladder. The room is stifling hot, with dim lighting and a lingering aroma that lures the students into a drowsy stupor. Harry's immediate impression of Professor Trelawney is that of a *large, glittering insect.* [2] She floats about the room making airy predictions each class session, including the immediate and persistent prediction that Harry will soon meet his demise. Not the easiest first day of lessons for a thirteen-year-old. While some students develop a cult following of Professor

Trelawney, others like Hermione come to loathe her near-fraudulent assertions. Even among J.K. Rowling's cast of eccentric characters, Professor Trelawney is truly unique.

✳ MELODRAMATIC ✳

I always pictured Professor Trelawney as buzzing around the classroom from student to student, trying to impress upon them the importance of her subject and soak up their admiration. She begins her first lesson with an animated introduction:

> *"You may not have seen me before. I find that descending too often into the hustle and bustle of the main school clouds my Inner Eye."*

She pauses for dramatic effect as everyone silently stares back at her:

> *"So you have chosen to study Divination, the most difficult of all magical arts. I must warn you at the outset that if you do not have the Sight, there is very little I will be able to teach you."*

I want to take this moment to remind you that Professor Trelawney is sitting on a winged armchair in front of a flaming fire in an attempt to create an intimidating and mysterious atmosphere.

> *"Many witches and wizards, talented though they are in the area of loud bangs and smells and sudden disappearings, are yet unable to penetrate the veiled mysteries of the future...It is a Gift granted to few. You, boy,"* she said suddenly to Neville, who almost toppled off his pouf. *"Is your grandmother well?"*
>
> *"I think so,"* said Neville tremulously.
>
> *"I wouldn't be so sure if I were you, dear,"*

Professor Trelawney just went out of her way to tell Neville something is terribly wrong with his grandmother, the woman who raised him. How can she expect him to pay attention for the rest of class? He doesn't have any means to check and see if she is okay. There are no cell phones at Hogwarts. If this were the Muggle world, I wouldn't blame him if he was frantically texting her under his desk to check in. She seems unconcerned by his terror, however, and continues with her introduction of Divination:

> *"The first term will be devoted to reading the tea leaves. Next term we shall progress to palmistry. By the way, my dear," she shot suddenly at Parvati Patil, "beware a red-haired man."*

This accusation causes Parvati to give Ron a frightened look and scoot her chair further away from him. Now she's making her students suspicious of their classmates. Great.

> *"And around Easter, one of our number will leave us forever."*

What does this mean? One of them will be dead? Who says this? Trelawney then turns her attention to Lavender, who has a look of terror and I don't blame her for being freaked out by now. So far Professor Trelawney has told a student his grandmother is not well, another that a red-haired man is going to attack her, and the whole class that one of them could possibly die before the year is up or worse, be expelled. But she's relieved when all Trelawney asks is to pass her a teapot. Seemingly safe, Lavender hands her the teapot and then Trelawney says *"Incidentally, that thing you are dreading — it will happen on Friday the sixteenth of October."* Oh wait, there's the traumatic prediction Lavender was hoping to avoid.

And to wrap up her introduction, Professor Trelawney takes advantage of and amplifies Neville's nervousness in order to demonstrate her own abilities by asking him *"After you've broken your first cup, would you be so kind as to select one of the blue patterned ones?"* She is deliberately manipulating her students. This introduction lasts, what, five minutes? In a short time span she already makes the majority of the class worried about illnesses, attacks and death.

The drama continues later in class as she overhears Ron talking about the sheep he sees in the bottom of Harry's tea cup:

> *"My dear," Professor Trelawney's huge eyes opened dramatically, "you have the Grim....The giant, spectral dog that haunts churchyards! My dear boy, it is an omen— the worst omen — of death!"* [3]

Unlike Slughorn's theatrics, Professor Trelawney's dramatic moments come at the expense of her students. Professor Slughorn uses exaggerated pauses and inflections to catch his students' attention and get them more involved in the learning process. Professor Trelawney just manipulates the students in order to prove her prowess in Divination. She correctly reads Neville's nervousness and uses this to her advantage. And as Hermione points out, Harry's past is well known. Here is a person in her classroom who has an obvious enemy. She uses this to her benefit in predicting an omen of death in his future. Of course the rest of the class is going to believe this, Harry has been close to death multiple times every year he's been at Hogwarts. This is successful in gaining their attention, and in some cases their admiration, but Professor Trelawney clearly does not think about how this will affect them.

Harry has his first Transfiguration lesson of the year immediately following this encounter with Professor Trelawney. He walks in frightened and bewildered. He sits in the back and tries to avoid everyone else's gaze and his own stray thoughts. When Professor McGonagall tells them about Animagi and transforms into a cat, Harry doesn't even notice, still shocked by Professor Trelawney's revelations. Harry is distressed. He thinks he saw the Grim just weeks before and here is a teacher confirming this death omen. Only when Professor McGonagall makes a joke about him not needing to turn in his homework if he's dead does he start to break of this worry. I don't think Professor Trelawney wants Harry to be afraid or to become unproductive the rest of the day, she simply wants to impress her students. But intentions hardly matter when consequences happen regardless.

* INADEQUATE *

Professor Trelawney's need to be manipulative and melodramatic stems from her inability to make accurate predictions. We know that Professor Trelawney has the ability to make true prophecies, including the one that causes Harry to be targeted by Lord Voldemort in the first place, but Trelawney herself is unaware of the prophecies she has revealed. She lives in a world where she feels completely inadequate. All her life she's been trying to recapture the legacy of her famous Seer ancestors. Suddenly she finds herself teaching the very subject. She takes the saying 'fake it until you make it' to heart.

Perhaps due to her feelings of inadequacy, Professor Trelawney secludes herself from the rest of the Hogwarts staff. When she does emerge from her tower, she overcompensates and becomes defensive, alienating her colleagues further. If she was willing to accept a little help in her classroom or befriend just one other teacher on campus she may have been able to learn how to soften her approach and create a safe learning environment.

Professor McGonagall is particularly turned off to Professor Trelawney's antics. In the first Transfiguration lesson of their third year, it takes all of Professor McGonagall's effort to not completely discredit Divination and Professor Trelawney's methods. Later in *Prisoner of Azkaban*, Professor Trelawney shockingly decides to join everyone for Christmas dinner. As Professor Dumbledore conjures up a chair for her to join the table she exclaims "*If I join the table, we shall be thirteen! Nothing could be more unlucky!*" Professor McGonagall becomes impatient and dismisses her worries, telling her they will risk it. Professor Trelawney eventually sits down and asks where Professor Lupin is. Dumbledore explains that Lupin is sick, again. When McGonagall questions Trelawney's ability to see the future, she replies *"Certainly I knew, Minerva...But one does not parade the fact that one is All-Knowing. I frequently act as though I am not possessed of the Inner Eye, so as not to make others nervous."*

As much as I love Professor McGonagall and her dry sense of humor, when she tells Trelawney *"That explains a great deal,"*[4] it reminds me of all those moments in my first few years of teaching where I felt so utterly alone. Most days I avoided the teacher's lounge because I felt unworthy. I felt like I couldn't show my face around veteran teachers, I'd be laughed at once they realized I had no idea what I was doing. I imagine it took a great deal of self-convincing for Professor Trelawney to actually make her way downstairs on Christmas to join the remaining staff and students. Granted, she doesn't make it easy for people to like her when she's constantly making false exclamations and calls herself 'all-knowing,' but I can't help to think that if Professor McGonagall had been more welcoming, maybe Professor Trelawney would have felt more at ease. Maybe she wouldn't have felt the need to defend her status and act like she's the best Seer in the world. She might have even picked up some tips from the other teachers as she got to know them and learn from their teaching styles. Professor McGonagall shows compassion and comes to her aid in *Order of the Phoenix* when Professor Umbridge tries to kick her out of the castle, but by that point it is too late, she has already lost her position because of the shortcomings in her teaching.

✳ ✳ ✳

Similar to Professor Trelawney, I am constantly plagued with feelings of inadequacy. In my first year of teaching, every little thing students said about me and my teaching abilities bothered me. Once, a student told me I looked like a raccoon because of the bags under my eyes and it took weeks to get over this tiny, stupid comment. I especially feared criticism from my coworkers. Any time another staff member or administrator walked in my room, I felt like I had to perform. I had to prove to them I was worthy. Professor Trelawney feels this same way when Professor Umbridge evaluates her classroom in *Order of the Phoenix*. Instead of being confident in her knowledge, she begins to exaggerate and make an even further fool of herself, fabricating a prediction about Umbridge,*"Why, I sense something... something dark... some grave peril..."*[5] This only leads to a bland smile and raised eyebrows. I've been there. I've had moments where I felt I had to make up for some imagined shortcoming. All this does is make it more apparent to those observing us that we're not confident in our abilities.

When I was first told I would be teaching Advanced Placement students, for a moment I was excited, I would finally be teaching the better behaved students. Like Ravenclaws, these students would be more interested in learning. Then I pictured Ravenclaw students sitting in front of me and I imagined them asking me difficult questions, ones I couldn't answer or didn't know the solution to. I began to freak out. Like Trelawney, I was concerned that I would be seen as a fraud. I admitted these feelings to a friend, who is the closest embodiment of these imaginary Ravenclaws I could find. She is the type of person who isn't afraid to prove anybody wrong, including her wealthy corporate boss. She told me, "I think one of the best skills to teach is how to be wrong gracefully and address mistakes productively. Students who know how to constructively challenge an authority figure will be the valued employees who keep their bosses from making expensive mistakes. If you want it to be structured, you could have a procedure for disagreeing with you. It would be a great model for them to take with them and a good skill set to practice." Valerie isn't a teacher, but she understood, better than me, that these were skills students needed to be taught. I had forgotten that it was natural for people to make mistakes. Students need to see a gracious response when they find the courage to correct an authority figure. Although this is a constant challenge, this was the reminder I needed to find the Gryffindor in me, be brave and get over the fact that I would make mistakes.

Professor Trelawney also lets students' criticism get under her skin. As Trelawney is in the middle of making another prediction of seeing the Grim, this time in Harry's crystal ball, Hermione explodes *"Oh for goodness' sake! Not that ridiculous Grim again!"* I'm curious to know what is going through Trelawney's mind as this point. Is she hurt? Does she fear being exposed as a fraud? Is this interjection striking at some deep-rooted insecurity? Whatever she is feeling, her response is unacceptable:

> *"I am sorry to say that from the moment you have arrived in this class, my dear, it has been apparent that you do not have what the noble art of Divination requires. Indeed, I don't remember ever meeting a student whose mind was so hopelessly mundane."*[6]

A student pointing out our inadequacies, while embarrassing, is no reason to throw back an insult. This pointed language pushes Hermione over the edge. She hastily gets up and leaves the class, never returning to a Divination lesson again. Hermione is already under a lot of stress at this point with the additional class load, and Professor Trelawney could have definitely handled this better.

To some extent I feel sorry for Professor Trelawney. She has a desire to be a great Seer yet lacks the ability to become one. I'm curious how she would respond to a student who was naturally gifted. I get the feeling this student would only make her feel more inadequate. Trelawney would never let a student succeed if it meant making herself look bad in comparison.

When Professor Trelawney does make mistakes, she isn't willing to admit them. During one lesson, she inaccurately predicts Harry's birthday as midwinter and the class begins to laugh. Instead of moving past this or admitting she was wrong, this causes her to assign homework that will take them an entire month to complete.

Although I like to think myself a better teacher than Trelawney, I too am guilty of taking out my insecurities on my students. I was providing instructions for a group activity one day when one of my students started pushing buttons on his watch and making it beep loudly. I was already fed up from a long day by that point and told him to hand it to me.

He tried to explain, stuttering "But... I'm..." when I cut him off saying, "I don't want to hear your excuses. You can get your watch back after school." Pleased with myself, I moved back to the instructions and broke my students up into their groups shortly after.

Lucas came back to see me at the end of the day and I proceeded to lecture him about listening to my instructions. The whole time I was dangling his red watch in front of him just out of his reach. He stood patiently in front of me not saying a single word, looking slightly ashamed. I admit it, I was pleased with myself. I felt like I was getting the hang of this discipline thing.

Lucas apologized and I handed the red watch back to him. "What were you trying to do anyway?" I asked, trying to make polite conversation. He reached across my desk and grabbed the watch from me then said, "I was trying to set my stop watch for 15 minutes—I was the timer." My stomach dropped. I had assigned each of them roles in their groups. One of them was the timer. His job was to keep time for the group to make sure they finished all tasks in the appropriate time limit. I had lectured a student for a couple minutes about paying attention to instructions when he had just been trying to follow my instructions the whole time. I felt so stupid. My face turned slightly red and it was my turn to feel ashamed. I immediately apologized to Lucas and admitted I was wrong. I asked him why he didn't just explain what he was doing and he gently reminded me that he had tried. And he was right, again. I had cut him off and told him I didn't want to hear his explanation. Unlike Trelawney, however, I was willing to admit my mistakes and took this event to heart.

* * *

Divination is a subject that Harry increasingly needs as his quest to defeat Lord Voldemort grows imminent. It becomes the center of Voldemort's return as well as his plan for killing Harry. Without prophecies, Harry's life would be drastically different. And yet the way Trelawney teaches tarnishes the subject for Harry altogether. He falls asleep in class, dismisses her predictions and loathes her lessons before they even begin. Harry is far from the only student to suffer from her poor teaching style. Even Dumbledore admits he was reluctant to hire Trelawney, only bringing her on after witnessing her first ever true prophecy. Professor Trelawney's inherent flaws may cause a few basic teaching issues, but it is her attempts to overcorrect through manipulation, misinformation and outright inconsiderate behavior that truly define her shortcomings as a teacher and turn many of her students from the subject of Divination forever.

FIRENZE

UNCONVENTIONAL

"I set myself against what is lurking in this forest, Bane, yes, with humans alongside me if I must." [1]

DIVINATION

Harry meets Firenze during his first year while serving detention in the Forbidden Forest. While searching for a fallen unicorn, Harry stumbles across a hooded figure drinking unicorn blood. Knowing the mysterious creature is actually Lord Voldemort, the centaur Firenze hurries to rescue Harry and allows him to clamber onto his back, carrying him to safety. The rest of the centaurs view this as an insult to their race and believe Firenze has allowed Harry to treat him as a common mule. Even in the face of this criticism, Firenze is willing to leave his traditions behind in order to stand up for what he believes is right. This is the only interaction readers have with Firenze until four books later in *Order of the Phoenix* when he replaces Professor Trelawney as the new Divination teacher.

Firenze offers a whole new perspective on Divination in contrast to Professor Trelawney's teaching methods. Where Trelawney is manipulative and inadequate, Firenze is honest and knowledgeable. He understands the uniqueness of Divination and allows students to learn from their mistakes without consequence. His unconventional approach to the subject keeps students awestruck, yet focused.

✳ UNCONVENTIONAL ✳

The students are unsure of how to react to the news that Firenze is replacing Professor Trelawney as their teacher. Some are ecstatic, like Lavender and Parvati who find him attractive. Others like Harry and Ron are weary, but have an open mind.

As the students enter their new classroom on Firenze's first day they find themselves in shock. Divination is no longer held in the astronomy tower as it would be impossible for Firenze to climb the ladder. Instead, they are in a previously unused classroom on the ground floor that has been transformed to replicate the atmosphere of the forest:

> "The classroom floor had become springily mossy and trees were growing out of it; their leafy branches fanned across the ceiling and windows, so that the room was full of slating shafts of soft, dappled, green light. The students who had already arrived were sitting on the earthy floor with their backs resting against tree trunks or boulders, arms wrapped around their knees or folded across their chests, looking rather nervous."[2]

Similar to Firenze, I have had the experience of starting at a new school in the middle of the year. The teacher prior to my arrival had quit due to stress. These eighth grade students were rather proud of how quickly they had run out their previous teacher. When I walked in that first day and they saw how young I was, I swear they began to smile. I had grown a lot during my first year of teaching (not physically grown) but I was still only in my second year and was barely twenty-three-years old. Even though I assured them daily I was committed to teaching them, my students still took bets on when I would quit. Some of them bet as little as three days!

I immediately made sure myself and the students were in a new classroom. It was a lot of work to move all the supplies to the new room, but I felt it was imperative that we started fresh. New classroom—new rules. I was determined to not let them walk all over me like they had with their previous teacher. That new room gave me a fighting chance. The first thing these students would observe about me is my classroom environment. They took in the walls, the arrangement of seats and the posters and immediately knew I was going to be different than their previous teacher, whose teaching style most resembled Filch skulking about the castle nagging at students. One of the prominent posters many of them examined showed a hybrid of Harry and Voldemort, one half of each face, with the words "I think it's nice that Voldemort always waits until the end of the year to kill Harry. Despite his flaws, he really cares about Harry's education."

Firenze, like me, is put in a difficult situation where he has to start a class with a group of students who have already become accustomed to the previous teacher's methods. Not to mention he is starting during a period at Hogwarts where the government has the most control. He's already got a target on his back from Umbridge and now he has to win his students over too. I wonder if his students were betting how long it would take for Umbridge to kick him out?

Decorating a classroom is simultaneously exciting and overwhelming. The first time I was handed my keys I stepped into the empty room with the intention of setting up my classroom immediately. Instead, I stood in the doorway for several minutes, stared at the blank walls and forty desks pushed to one side of the room, then turned around and walked out. I did what any self-respecting adult does when they're overwhelmed—I called my mom. I couldn't wrap my head around any of it. I suddenly had a million decisions to make and they all seemed so important. Even decisions as small as where my posters should go. I needed expert help and moms just know things.

My mom calmed me down and we got to work. Once I started putting the desks in rows and realized it was probably helpful if they faced the whiteboard, the rest of the decisions fell into place. In the grand scheme of things, the locations of small items like the posters didn't matter. My students would still learn from me even if I had left out that poster of Volde-Harry. But I had to spend hours in this room and I wanted to feel comfortable. I wanted it to reflect my personality. Small additions such as the Harry Potter paraphernalia and the fluffy rug under my desk where I would rest my bare feet after school helped with the long hours planning lessons.

Even though I spent more time in the classroom than my students, I wanted them to feel comfortable in the room as well. I created a wall space strictly for displaying student work. Even now that I teach high school, my students love the recognition they get when their exemplary work is pinned up on the wall. It also helps students feel some ownership of the space. It is no longer just my classroom, but ours together. In this manner we are all responsible for taking care of it and abiding by the rules.

Firenze chooses a forest-themed classroom. Whether for comfort or instructional purposes, the environment helps students immediately realize that his class will be different from Trelawney's. In this room, students get a natural sense of mysterious power they're not meant to understand. His is not the only classroom at Hogwarts that reflects the personality of its teacher. Students walking into Professor Snape's classroom immediately get a sense of dark, quiet power. Professor Lockhart, a person who values himself over others, decorates his room with full size portraits of himself. Professor Flitwick on the other hand goes out of his way to make his students feel welcome and comfortable. One year he even decorates his classroom for Christmas with real fairies that look like shimmering lights. This is such a simple gesture but made their classroom feel much more like a community.

The environment in Firenze's forest classroom is not only crucial for distancing himself from the precedent set and the regiment he finds himself in, but also for setting the tone of the lessons he gives. He fully intends for the students to become absorbed in his lessons and think about the subject without the limits of pre-conceived notions. In this class students are often startled by the bell, forgetting entirely that they're still in the castle. In contrast to Professor Trelawney's classroom this is a literal breath of fresh air. Her class was stifling and students often fell asleep. Trelawney's environment hindered their learning whereas Firenze's complements it.

In addition to Firenze's unconventional approach to the classroom environment, he has unique methods of teaching Divination. Firenze's first lesson with the fifth years requires them to sit on the moss covered floor of the newly transformed classroom and observe the stars as he walks amongst them providing instructions. Parvati tries to point out the lessons that Trelawney has taught them about Astronomy and Firenze dismisses them as unimportant human accidents. He explains that centaurs are more interested in larger events. Harry describes his first lesson with Firenze as the most unusual he had ever attended:

> They did indeed burn sage and mallowsweet there on the classroom floor, and Firenze told them to look for certain shapes and symbols in the pungent fumes, but he seemed perfectly unconcerned that not one of them could see any of the signs he described, telling them that humans were hardly ever good at this, that it took centaurs years and years to become competent, and finished by telling them that it was foolish to put too much faith in such things anyway, because even centaurs sometimes read them wrongly. He was nothing like any human teacher Harry had ever had. His priority did not seem to be to teach them what he knew, but rather to impress

upon them that nothing, not even centaurs' knowledge was foolproof.[3]

Firenze's approach to such a fickle subject is refreshing especially in comparison to Professor Trelawney. In his classroom it is acceptable to not know the answer. In Trelawney's class, students were ridiculed for mistakes as simple as misidentifying shapes in their tea leaves. Firenze openly tells students that even the experts, centaurs who have been studying the planets' movements for years, still get information wrong. Because of his open approach to Divination and willingness to admit he makes mistakes, students feel more comfortable to ask questions and admit when they're unsure of the correct response. The mere suggestion would have provoked a dramatic reaction from Professor Trelawney.

✳ ✳ ✳

Firenze is a unique professor for both Harry and us to learn from. Not only does he bring a rare worldview as a centaur, but he also comes into Hogwarts willing to teach like no other professor before him. While students like Harry and Ron never go on to master Divination, his unfamiliar approach and engrossing classroom environment help to create a space where above all else, they are encouraged to grow as individuals.

PART III: CORE CLASSES

Madam Hooch

*

Professor Sinistra

*

Professor Binns

MADAM HOOCH

DIRECT

"Everyone stand by a broomstick. Come on, hurry up." [1]

FLYING LESSONS

Madam Hooch gets to teach an activity that I would absolutely love to try, fly a broomstick. What I don't envy is having to instruct a class of rowdy first years. She seems up for the task, however, when described as having *eyes like a hawk* [2] as she gazes upon her eager students. Her lesson is the closest we get to the students taking any sort of gym class at Hogwarts, and even then the most physical activity they accomplish is walking all the way out to the grounds for their lesson. Are students being taught proper nutrition and exercise? Sure, balanced meals are being provided and the moving staircases are a workout. But what happens when they leave Hogwarts and are able to Apparate any place they need to travel? Perhaps there's a spell to keep you in shape. Either way, outside of proper wand movement and dodging stray spells inside the classroom, flying is the only physical skill students are taught.

I hadn't realized that Madam Hooch is never referred to as 'professor' in the series until I started writing this book. Why isn't she given the same title as the other teachers? Perhaps she isn't given this status because her subject isn't quite as academic as the rest of the classes. In fact, in *Sorcerer's Stone* the students only find out about their first flying lesson through a notice pinned up in the Gryffindor common room. It seems like flying might not be considered a class so much as extra lessons that only first years are required to take. Even so, flying seems to be an important skill in the magical world. Outside of enjoyment on the Quidditch pitch, characters in the series frequently use flight as a means of travel and even escape. There are other ways of getting around, but flying seems to be the only method (other than Muggle forms) that isn't tracked by the Ministry of Magic. Obviously this skill is important for efficiency in the wizarding world and yet students only seem to receive one cut-short lesson in their first year.

∗ DIRECT ∗

In the books, there isn't a great deal of time dedicated to Madam Hooch aside from Harry's first flying lesson. I assume that she helps out around Hogwarts and gives the students more lessons after this first failed attempt, especially since the only person she actually saw get off the ground was Neville, who ended up in the hospital wing with a broken wrist. Let's walk through her one lesson together.

Harry walks out to the flat lawn on the grounds opposite the Forbidden Forest. The Gryffindors are paired up to take this lesson with (as is often the case) the Slytherins, making many of the first years apprehensive. Harry doesn't want to make a fool of himself in front of Malfoy and his gang.

There are twenty broomsticks waiting for them as they approach. So far, this is a good sign for Madam Hooch. It says a lot that her materials are already laid out in an orderly manner for her students. Immediately upon entering, it sets a precedent in her class that work is going to be done. It took me a year before I realized I needed something for my students to work on at the start of class. Now I require them to answer an opening question every day. It gives me time to take roll and get things situated and gives them something to do besides wander around the classroom and talk to their friends. This, however, requires me to have a question prepared and projected for each class before they enter.

As the Gryffindors and Slytherins are standing around, Madam Hooch arrives and she gets straight to business. The first words out of her mouth are *"Well, what are you waiting for? ... Everyone stand by a broomstick. Come on, hurry up."*[3] She doesn't even greet the students. She can't possibly know their names already, right? Shouldn't she discuss some rules or procedures? They're about to fly on broomsticks after all. Many of them never even knew flying broomsticks were real until recently. Instead, she just barks at them to move to either side of a broomstick.

Then she instructs them to stick their hand over their broomstick and say the word 'Up.' Harry's is one of the few broomsticks to immediately jump into his hand, but Neville's and Hermione's remain on the ground even after a considerable amount of effort. Harry thinks to himself that perhaps broomsticks, like many animals, can sense the fear in your voice. Madam Hooch, however, doesn't address any of their problems or concerns.

I will give her some credit here, Madam Hooch does a great job starting with something simple. And having the students shout at their brooms probably helps with the nerves. She should, however, explain to the students exactly why someone like Harry is able to call his broom immediately into his hand while others have more trouble.

She could have done this two ways: first, simply tell them beforehand that a broom can sense when you are afraid and will only respond to a steady voice. Second, go through this lesson exactly as she has done but afterwards ask the class why they think some were able to summon the broomsticks into their hands more quickly than others. This would give everyone the opportunity to think through the process just as Harry did and maybe even give him the opportunity to share his theory about broomsticks and horses. A student like Neville may still have difficulty keeping the fear out of his voice, but students of Hermione's caliber would take this to heart and perform better next time.

Madam Hooch then models how to mount and grip their broomsticks. This is a good skill to demonstrate. While some students like Ron have been watching Quidditch their whole life and think they know the proper technique, others like Harry and Hermione have never seen someone fly on a broomstick and would have no idea where to begin. This helps the students see the proper way before attempting flight and possibly making a fool of themselves.

She then tells students *"Now, when I blow my whistle, you kick off from the ground, hard, … Keep your brooms steady, rise a few feet, and then come back down by leaning forward slightly."* At this point, she should have, again, demonstrated exactly what she was looking for. If she had first modeled the behavior and showed the students exactly how she wanted them to push from the ground and hover for a moment, many more students would have been successful. Even if he still failed, Neville would have been more confident and perhaps improved his methods after seeing exactly what he was supposed to be mimicking. He would have been less nervous and would have pushed off with everyone else. Instead, Neville pushes off early and ends up falling several feet, breaking his wrist.

Neville needs to be taken to the hospital wing, so she turns to her class and instructs them to *"leave those brooms where they are or you'll be out of Hogwarts before you can say 'Quidditch.'"*[4] This is Madam Hooch's biggest mistake. I know, J.K. Rowling needed her to leave to move along the plot of her story, but no! Just no! One of her students just broke his wrist falling off a broom because of improper guidance. And now she leaves a group of twenty first years with broomsticks and zero guidance during their first lesson! Not to mention they are a bunch of Gryffindors and Slytherins, well known for their bitter rivalry.

I can understand leaving them alone if they are high school students who have some experience flying and will not fall off their brooms, or if she knows the students personally and knows for a fact that they will not disobey her direct orders. But she doesn't know them. I'm not sure she even knows their names yet. She's been with them all of about ten minutes, and they are eleven and want to prove themselves. Of course they are going to ride those brooms!

Up until this point, Madam Hooch had been doing a decent job with the first years. I wish we could have read more about her teaching experiences. She is present throughout all of Harry's school career monitoring Quidditch practices, refereeing matches, and I assume carrying on giving flying lessons. When teaching, Madam Hooch has a very direct style, always getting straight to the point. She occasionally models the activities well and has students practice the skills asked of them. For all we know, these egregious errors may have been the result of a bad day that she would go on to regret. From personal experience, it seems as if every teacher's worst day is the day they are observed. Perhaps it's the same for Madam Hooch. If strict Professor McGonagall still trusts Madam Hooch after catching her first year students left alone with twenty broomsticks then she's clearly doing something right.

PROFESSOR SINISTRA

UNKNOWN

"Professor Grubbly-Plank was chatting to Professor Sinistra, the Astronomy teacher..." [1]

ASTRONOMY

Professor Sinistra is—who again? Apparently she teaches Astronomy, one of the core subjects at Hogwarts and yet we never see a single one of her lessons. We do hear Harry, Ron and Hermione discuss her homework on a few occasions but little else. How unremarkable do you have to be to teach a class in the middle of the night, yet never do anything worth mentioning? Clearly her style of teaching has no impact on her students, and because of this the only lesson we can learn from her is that we should, at the very least, do something memorable in our classes once in a while.

PROFESSOR BINNS

DULL * DETACHED

"My subject is History of Magic," he said in his dry, wheezy voice. "I deal with facts, Miss Granger, not myths and legends."[1]

HISTORY OF MAGIC

Professor Binns teaches History of Magic, where students get the opportunity to study magical creatures, wars and the development of the wizarding community. Sounds exciting, right? Well, not for Harry and his friends. Professor Binns takes material that we would pay to see in a movie theater and makes it so incredibly boring that only students as diligent as Hermione listen to his lectures each day.

We all have had a teacher like this, one so dull that even the fact that Professor Binns is a ghost does little to make him intriguing. Binns is described as being so old and mundane that one day *"he had fallen asleep in front of the staff room fire and got up the next morning to teach, leaving his body behind him,"[2]* as if nothing had changed. And Harry thinks, *"The most exciting thing that ever happened in his classes was his entering the room through the blackboard."[3]* Perhaps Professor Binns was a better teacher when alive, but in death he fails to captivate and connect with his students.

✳ DULL ✳

As a history teacher I am offended by Professor Binns' representation of history classes. At my school, the history teachers are some of the most animated and humorous people I have ever encountered. As a department, we enjoy our time with each other and with our students. This love for our profession transfers back into the classroom. Our department has a good reputation and students generally love coming to our classes. This is not the case for all history teachers. Sometimes students are so turned off from history by the time they reach our classes that it takes extra effort to keep them engaged.

Unlike the history teachers at my school site, Professor Binns' teaching style is so boring that students come to hate History of Magic almost instantly. Professor Binns' sole method of teaching is through direct, inattentive instruction causing the classes to feel monotonous. Time spent in his classroom is almost as soul-sucking as the halls of Azkaban. Students fall asleep in his class every day and he doesn't notice. While it is true that History of Magic is one of the few subjects taught at Hogwarts without magic, studying giant wars and bloody goblin riots should be engrossing if taught the right way.

Clearly the issue is not the content. My students love studying the World Wars. They're fascinated by the decisions people make throughout history to fight for what they believe in. The issue lies in Professor Binns' teaching style. Students like Hermione would never fail to miss a word from any professor's mouth, but the majority of students can't handle what is essentially reciting a textbook day after day.

My high school history teacher would stand at his podium with an outline of the main topics of the day written in marker behind him then proceed to go over each bullet point one at a time until the bell rang at the end of class. From this description alone he sounds similar to Professor

Binns. In actuality, he stood at that podium every day and engaged students by turning history into a thrilling tale. The way he connected events and tied people's struggles to the main events in history was fascinating. I felt like I was listening to a captivating audiobook for fifty minutes a day. This is when I really began to fall in love with history. This worked for my teacher, but it doesn't work for Professor Binns because he doesn't have this same ability to engage an audience.

As someone who dislikes talking for long periods of time, lecturing does not come naturally to me either. And while I am opposed to lecturing every day, sometimes a good lecture is needed to get through the many standards we are required to cover and note taking is a great skill for students to learn. Even so, I had to experiment to find out how to make note taking more enjoyable for myself and my students. In order to achieve effective lectures, I need to include pictures and videos to help break up the monotony. This gives me a break from talking and helps students with different learning modalities connect to the material. Sometimes I only include the title and pictures as a way to force students to listen, write in their own words and practice synthesizing the most important information to include in their notes. I also try to make the lecture more interactive by asking students open-ended questions periodically. This helps me check for understanding and keep students engaged.

Even with these additions, I find my lectures still lack an extra element that a performer like Professor Slughorn can naturally bring to a lecture. When I first taught students about the American Revolutionary War using a traditional lecture they didn't seem to grasp the enormity of the opposition the colonists were attempting to defeat. I decided to take a different approach the following year. I had my students take notes on the Pre-War Statistics. I gave them a paper with two blank football helmets facing each other and told them to label one colonists and the other side redcoats. They decorated the helmets to their liking and then I had them make predictions about the war based on the statistics I provided. As I lectured, they filled in a chart for each side: we compared the generals (who became the quarterbacks), the number of soldiers (players) each side had, the differences in uniforms and weapons. They wrote down each side's nicknames and even who the supporters (fans) of each side were. Then at the end of the notes they had to make a prediction on which team they thought would win. These notes also included some Monday Night Football music to add to the effect.

My students absolutely loved the comparison to football teams because it was something they could easily understand. Most predicted that the British would win which made it even more fascinating for them when later in the unit we got to the reasons why the colonists were able to win independence. The cohesive focus on the football metaphor helped students focus and retain the information more effectively than the previous year's simple lecture. In comparison to Professor Binns' lecture in *Sorcerer's Stone*, when he *"droned on and on while they scribbled down names and dates, and got Emeric the Evil and Uric the Oddball mixed up,"*[4] I think most students would prefer the more interactive method of note taking.

Another one of Professor Binns's problems lies in the delivery of his lessons. J.K. Rowling describes his teaching style as *monotonous* and *guaranteed to cause severe drowsiness.*[5] Teaching about giants, wizards and goblins is subject matter that absolutely should be interesting. Our style of speaking should add more to our lessons than it takes away. But in Professor Binns's class it does just the opposite—what was once exciting material is now a dreaded lecture.

A teacher's voice is crucial in the delivery of material. When I was first becoming a teacher I had so many people tell me "just wait until you get your teacher's voice." "You'll be great once you find your teaching voice." How do you find a voice? If I was getting a new voice I'd hope it would allow me to sing without sounding like a banshee. I was sure I was never going to find this so-called voice. Surely they just meant I had to be louder, so louder I became. And it worked! I had found my true teaching voice. I was definitely an official teacher now just like all those people had said. Well, that's what I thought.

In my second year of teaching, my principal evaluated one of my lessons and I thought it went brilliantly. She agreed for the most part, but towards the end of our post-evaluation meeting she mentioned that my voice was very loud. As someone who is frequently seen as the quietest one in the room I was pleasantly surprised with this comment. Then she mentioned, "You must be tired by the end of the day." Sensing a trap, I slowly nodded my head and she continued, "You should try and lower your voice and quietly get their attention. This way if you do need to raise your voice they will notice." I left her office upset and in denial. Of course my voice was loud, I was teaching thirty-eight seventh graders the meaning of capitalism by simulating a variation of Roller Coaster Tycoon. I had to be loud.

The next period, I continued to reflect on her comments. Inside I knew I needed to accept her criticism, but outwardly I was upset. I thought my lesson was brilliant, why couldn't she see that I had things under control? Eventually I gave in and practiced lowering my voice and, as much as I hated to admit it at the time, she was right. Students were less likely to talk over me if I was using a calmer tone of voice. While this won't always work, I've found it to be a subtle game-changer.

Professor Binns doesn't have the same volume issue but his monotone voice is a primary factor in hindering students' learning. His class is described again in *Chamber of Secrets*:

> *"Professor Binns opened his notes and began to read in a flat drone like an old vacuum cleaner until nearly everyone in the class was in a deep stupor, occasionally coming to long enough to copy down a name or date, then falling asleep again."*[6]

If Binns had attempted to make his lectures more exciting or changed the tone of his voice every once in a while he might have found the right balance for his students to properly learn in his classroom.

✳ DETACHED ✳

Professor Binns is so removed from his classes that he doesn't even know his students' names. I understand that he is literally detached from the physical world, but if Nearly Headless Nick can do it, so can he. In *Order of the Phoenix* he calls Harry by the name *"Perkins."*[7] Seriously? Harry is one of the most famous people in the wizarding world, if not the *most* famous and after five years in his class, Professor Binns doesn't even know his name. He's a wizarding history teacher for crying out loud. He does the same to Hermione in *Chamber of Secrets*, prompting her for her name and then calling her by the wrong name mere seconds later. If Professor Binns doesn't even try to learn his students' names, how can he possibly expect them to respect him?

Building relationships with our students is one of the most important things we can do as teachers. I try to learn my students' names as quickly as I can in the beginning of the school year. With about 185 new students each year it can be a tough task. I usually have them mastered by the end of the first week, but until then I study the seating chart and quiz myself when standing in front of the class. I warn my students beforehand that if they feel like I'm staring at them unnecessarily that I promise I'm not a creeper, I'm just trying to memorize their names and faces. They appreciate the effort, and I think they appreciate the warning too.

It is also imperative that we learn the correct pronunciation of students' names. When I was a student, I was so afraid to speak up and tell teachers that I actually preferred Dani to Danielle. I just hoped they would figure it out after I wrote Dani on my papers all year. Some did and others did not. I never felt like I built a relationship with the teachers that called me Danielle. They didn't bother to get to know the real me.

Ask your students and some of them will tell you how often they have had teachers call them by the incorrect name or wrong pronunciation. One year, I had a transgender student in class who preferred a different name to the one given at birth. This student also wanted to be referred to not as he or she, but they and them. Some teachers had difficulty complying. This bright student would get very upset and shutdown if referred to as something other than what they identified with. I tried my best to refer to them just by the name they chose instead of overthinking the pronouns and accidentally misgendering them. When I did mess up, other students would correct me or this student would visibly flinch and I would correct myself. Even with the mistakes, I know that the effort was appreciated. We were able to develop a good relationship because I respected their choices. Professor Binns not taking the time to learn his students' names sends them a message that he doesn't care about them as individuals. The same is true in our classrooms. How can we expect our students to learn anything from us if we don't bother to learn their names? Their real names.

In contrast to Professor Binns, even the owner of the ice cream parlor in Diagon Alley does a better job of teaching history while developing a relationship with Harry. Florean Fortescue supplied free ice cream and would discuss key events while Harry worked on his summer homework for History of Magic. Almost a year later, while taking the exam, Harry thinks back to what Fortescue taught him, having learned more about medieval witch burnings from a few sunny afternoons outside the ice cream shop with Florean Fortescue than a whole year under Professor Binns's instruction. I'm sure Harry would credit the ice cream for the retention of the material but the real credit goes to Fortescue. His willingness to go out of his way to get to know Harry and discuss his homework helped him retain the material better than any of Professor Binns' detached lectures.

* * *

In addition to refusing to develop relationships with his students, Professor Binns doesn't even notice obvious distractions in his classroom such as when Harry gets up, opens the window and lets Hedwig into the class in *Order of the Phoenix*. Harry finds himself in his usual stupor when Hermione jabs him in the ribs and points towards the window. Hedwig is standing on the window sill and is visibly injured. Harry raises his hand, Professor Binns calls him by the wrong name again, and he asks to go to the hospital wing. Binns barely notices Harry's question and completely fails to notice that an owl has now appeared in his class. Can you imagine? An actual owl is in his class, every single students' attention is on Hedwig and not him, and he has absolutely no idea.

I can't say I'm completely innocent of such occurrences since I had a similar experience in my fifth year of teaching. Towards the end of the year I was standing on a chair to put away some boxes on top of the cabinets. As I was climbing down I noticed a penny stuck to the wall just above my eye level. Intrigued, I moved the chair over and pulled at the sticky penny. I had caught the attention of a few students and commented out loud, "How did a penny get stuck up here?" One student laughed and said, "You didn't know it was there?" She told me that three months before two boys had a competition to see who could get the penny to stick the highest on the wall. They were jumping up and down in the back of the room and I had never even noticed. Like Binns, I was unaware of what was occurring in my own class. This was a good reminder that I needed to be more aware of my surroundings. There are moments throughout the day when I become so focused on grading papers or designing lessons that I forget students are always sitting in front of me needing my attention.

Easily the best teaching moment Professor Binns has in all seven books is when he agrees to tell the second years about the Chamber of Secrets. Though it does take Hermione pestering him about it before he finally gives in and tells the story, for once in his death he delivers a lesson that none of his students would forget. For the first time, I'm sure, in a long time, he has everyone's attention. There is a sense of unease as all eyes are on him, soaking up every word. As soon as he finishes telling the story of the Chamber of Secrets, Seamus, Parvati and Dean all ask additional questions. However, he quickly becomes annoyed by these extra inquiries and returns to his usual teaching method as the class sinks back to sleep.

Early on in my teaching career, I was observing an eleventh grade U.S. History teacher who was teaching a lesson on the Civil Rights Movement of the 1960s. The teacher was talking about the impact slavery had in the South and mentioned the Civil War. He asked the students if they knew who fought in this major war. Many responded with absurd answers, ranging from Great Britain to Germany and much more. The majority of these students had no idea that the Civil War was an internal conflict. The teacher simply told them the answer and continued on with his lecture on Civil Rights.

Another student raised his hand and asked what the conflict was about and the teacher replied, "You were supposed to learn all about the Civil War in 8th grade. We need to stick to what is on our standards." I was shocked. Sitting in front of him was a class of sixteen and seventeen-year-olds who were curious to know more about one of the United States' biggest conflicts and yet he denied them this learning opportunity. Not to mention, this is essential for them to understand further topics and concepts in United States History, particularly the Civil Rights Movement. I vowed to never do this to my students. Sometimes as teachers we have so much pressure from administration to teach to the test or teach to the standards that we forget to teach for the students.

Professor Binns would have had much better results in his classroom if he would realize that the reason he floats into class every day is not to lecture to an empty room but to teach actual living students—a good reminder for us all.

* * *

Although most of this chapter has been harping on poor old Professor Binns, these practices are unfortunately common in our school systems. It is important for our students to learn how to take good notes and be prepared for college but lecturing every day in this dull and detached manner will lead to bright but easily distracted students like Harry and Ron relying on Hermione's notes to get by. Professor Binns does make many teaching mistakes, but he is still very knowledgeable. While I'm not sure exactly how old he is, he definitely has lived through more history than his students so he'd better know his material! Regardless, it is a very important trait to have.

While Professor Binns is a well-educated teacher, his other characteristics hinder the students from learning in his class. Only intense students similar to Hermione are going to be successful in this environment. With some variation and added enthusiasm, however, History of Magic could become a class the students would look forward to attending. As it stands, Professor Binns is an immaterial version of a teacher, and it is appropriate that he is referred to as *"the ghost of Professor Binns"*[8] and not simply 'professor.'

PART IV: DEFENSE AGAINST THE DARK ARTS

PROFESSOR QUIRRELL

*

PROFESSOR LOCKHART

*

PROFESSOR LUPIN

*

PROFESSOR MOODY

*

PROFESSOR UMBRIDGE

PROFESSOR QUIRRELL

NERVOUS

"D-Defense Against the D-D-Dark Arts," muttered Professor Quirrell, as though he'd rather not think about it. [1]

DEFENSE AGAINST THE DARK ARTS

Defense Against the Dark Arts is the core subject taught at Hogwarts where students learn to defend themselves against vicious magical attacks. Along with counter-spells, students are supposed to learn defensive dueling techniques and protections against dark creatures. Unlike most other subjects, this course is critical to their survival in the magical world. No professor, however, has held the post longer than a year since Lord Voldemort asked for the job himself, feeding into rumors that he jinxed the position. We see seven teachers in seven years fill the role of Defense Against the Dark Arts professor, the first being Quirinus Quirrell who takes on the position in *Sorcerer's Stone* after a brief sabbatical.

Harry is passing through the Leaky Cauldron on his way to buy school supplies when he meets Professor Quirrell. He has just been told he is a wizard, he's walking with a literal giant into a secret pub and he's shaking all kinds of strange people's hands. Not only has he just learned that he can do magic, now he finds out he is one of the most famous wizards of all time. Can you imagine how overwhelming that would be for an eleven-year-old? And I thought just transferring to a new school was hard. In this moment Harry meets his first magical teacher. This is a chance for Professor Quirrell to make him feel comfortable and welcome in this world. Instead, Quirrell appears even more nervous than Harry, stuttering through almost every word and doing absolutely nothing to reassure him.

While this is Professor Quirrell's first year as the Defense Against the Dark Arts teacher, it is not his first year teaching. From a professional standpoint, there is no excuse for how nervous he is all the time. Yes, he has Voldemort on the back of his head—and I imagine that would be extremely nerve-racking—but for the sake of this book we are mostly going to concentrate on his teaching abilities. Quirrell may not be the worst teacher that the Hogwarts students have had to endure, but he quickly sets a low bar for Defense Against the Dark Arts.

✳ NERVOUS ✳

Professor Quirrell, a former Ravenclaw student, was intelligent but lacked self-esteem and was teased endlessly. J.K. Rowling writes that he developed an interest in the Dark Arts and sought out Lord Voldemort as a way to make people take notice. It's no secret that Voldemort attracted fearful admiration from all but the most powerful of wizards. Even Ollivander can't help but remark about his power: *"[he] did great things — terrible, yes, but great."*[2] Seeking this type of praise, Quirrell (literally) attaches himself to Voldemort's achievements. I understand Quirrell's desire to fit in, but attaching an evil growth to the back of your head really isn't the best way to achieve greatness.

I wonder if Quirrell was a better teacher before he aligned himself with Voldemort. Instead of finding personal success, now he's more nervous and mocked than ever. He comes to fear everyone and lets his emotions affect his teaching abilities. Sure, his stammering serves to direct suspicion at the bully Professor Snape—successfully, I might add—but it is his nervousness that prevents his students from learning. There's no reason you can't teach great lessons and attempt to steal the Sorcerer's Stone at the same time.

As an introvert prone to nervousness, the first day of school is one of the hardest days of the year for me. I enjoy meeting all my new students, but I hate having to meet all these new students. Does that make sense? I find the awkward first day procedures and testing of the waters torturous. I want to skip straight to the part where I know all my students' names and interests and get right to the subject matter. Unfortunately that's not possible, making the first interaction we have with our students crucial in setting the tone for the rest of the school year. Professor Quirrell's first interaction with Harry plays out like this:

> "P-P-Potter," stammered Professor Quirrell, grasping Harry's hand, "c-can't t-tell you how p-pleased I am to meet you."
>
> "What sort of magic do you teach, Professor Quirrell?"
>
> "D-Defense Against the D-D-Dark Arts," muttered Professor Quirrell, as though he'd rather not think about it. "N-not that you n-need it, eh, P-P-Potter?"[3]

In the movie version of this meeting, Harry is calm and excited to meet his professor for the first time, even initiating the interaction by sticking out his hand for Quirrell to shake. But Quirrell just stares at Harry's hand like it's Nagini about to bite him. Even though I constantly have social anxiety ads popping up on my Facebook feed (seriously Facebook, this doesn't make people feel better) this doesn't mean I would react like Professor Quirrell does upon first meeting Harry. On the first day of school I have structures in place to help avoid this awkwardness. As my students enter the classroom, I hand them a short questionnaire where they write down their favorite book, show, candy, etc. This eliminates the sweaty handshake and gives students something to do rather than just sit there twirling their thumbs before moving on to an interactive lesson where they get to know me. While we don't get to see Quirrell's first day procedures, I'm sure they were just as awkward as this initial encounter in the Leaky Cauldron.

We never get a full view of what Quirrell is like as a teacher, but what we do see isn't flattering. In *Sorcerer's Stone* many of the students were excited for Defense Against the Dark Arts classes but mention that *"Quirrell's lessons turned out to be a bit of a joke."*[4] One of the only mentions of a Defense Against the Dark Arts lesson in *Sorcerer's Stone* is when they're forced to copy down different ways to treat werewolf bites, presumably straight from a textbook. We do briefly glimpse him in the classroom in the movie version of *Sorcerer's Stone*. All we see are a few seconds of him standing on a stage in front of his class holding what looks to be a lizard of some sort. An iguana? I'm not sure. I'm a history teacher not a lizard expert! And, to top this off, I'm not even sure where the lizard (iguana?) could possibly come into this lesson since he's discussing vampire bats at the time. I played the clip back a couple of times to check the subtitle's accuracy and was entirely bored within just three-seconds of his nervous stuttering, a sentiment I'm sure his students shared.

As I think back on my teaching experience, I realize I have had many stuttering Professor Quirrell moments. Once while teaching about World War II in the Pacific, I meant to say 'The Japanese continued fighting no matter what was thrown at them.' But what I ended up saying was "The Japanese continued farting..." I tried to continue like nothing happened except that one student who notices everything spoke up and asked "Did you just say farting, Ms. Dickie?" Yes, yes I did. And it wasn't the last time. Another year I accidentally combined the words drastic and dramatic, saying "dramastic." It became our class's new made-up word to describe anything exciting. But the worst mistake came during a discussion on the Civil Rights Movement when I accidentally substituted the word 'protestors' with 'prostitutes.' What separates me from Professor Quirrell, however, is my willingness to admit mistakes and laugh along with my students. Rather than make me appear weak, these slip-ups helped me grow closer to them.

Professor Quirrell further exhibits his weakness by letting students and other teachers push him around. The Weasley twins even bewitch snowballs to bounce off the back of his turban (if you think about it, they were essentially throwing snowballs at Lord Voldemort). They are penalized for this behavior, but I would be surprised if Quirrell was the one to punish them. It's far more likely that Professor McGonagall happened to be in the vicinity and gave them detention herself.

Quirrell also manages to make the entire school panic with just a few untimely words about an escaped troll. Let's ignore the fact that Quirrell is the one to let in the troll and actually wants chaos to ensue. This *is* his goal and it does work. As a teacher, however, he does the worst possible thing for the students by running into the Great Hall and shouting out *"Troll — in the dungeons — thought you ought to know."*[5] This, of course, causes everyone to panic and it's not until Dumbledore sends firecrackers into the air that students realize they need to file out in a composed manner.

In these emergency situations I find it's best to remain calm, which can be extremely hard depending on the circumstances. One year on the third day of school, I heard over the loudspeaker "teachers and staff we are now on a lockdown." Fortunately my class was quiet at the time, so I could clearly hear the addition "this is not a drill." After locking the door and turning out the lights, I told my students it was probably just a precaution and continued lecturing on the founding fathers to set them at ease. We were on the second floor far from the incident so my students were safe, but in contrast to Quirrell's panicked response, a simple matter-of-fact demeanor kept them calm.

✳ ✳ ✳

Professor Quirrell is a good reminder to not let dark forces get to our heads. His nervousness overwhelms him and negatively impacts his effectiveness as a teacher. The greatest cause of Quirrell's nerves stems from a parasitic Lord Voldemort controlling his actions from under the turban, but mine is inside my own mind. At the same age Harry bravely stood up to Quirrell-mort, my parents had to force me to try out for soccer, a sport I already loved. I still get nervous in new situations like back-to-school nights or even small acts such as driving people to new locations, but now I can somewhat combat nervousness with over-preparation.

On days when my insides are squirming, prior to students' (or administrators') arrival I will walk around the room picking up stray papers or straightening the textbooks. This movement helps get the blood flowing and focuses my mind on other things. I set routines for the beginning of the class period, such as warm-ups, which help give me a minute to breathe and prepare for the day. And creating detailed presentations or lessons helps me rely on notes to guide instruction, putting less emphasis on my delivery of information as the only means of student success.

Prior to my very first day of teaching, after several days of planning the day down to the minute, I actually wrote a blog post titled "Calm before the storm?" On my most nervous day, I was so prepared that I was questioning my calmness. I find preparation helpful, but sometimes it's necessary to just trudge along and take stressful situations one at a time. In *Half-Blood Prince*, Dumbledore explains that even though their duel is foretold, Harry has a choice and doesn't have to face Voldemort. Even so, their encounter is inevitable because Voldemort will never quit hunting him. Harry realizes that with or without the prophecy, he would want to be the one to finish Voldemort, thinking to himself: *"It was the difference between being dragged in the arena to face a battle to the death and walking into the arena with your head held high."*[6] This advice is what keeps me going when dealing with nerves. They are going to be there no matter what I am doing, so I might as well face them head on. In the end, I try to remember that it's not about me but my students, and that's what helps me prevail.

Quirrell's students were so excited to take Defense Against the Dark Arts. It's disappointing that he fails to live up to their expectations and lets his insecurities get in the way of the simple joys of the subject matter. Only Umbridge approved of his lessons, saying none of their previous teachers would have passed a ministry evaluation *"with the possible exception of Professor Quirrell, who did at least appear to have restricted himself to age-appropriate subjects."[7]* If Umbridge praises his theory-based approach to teaching, you know that can't mean he was doing anything riveting in the classroom. Hagrid's description of Professor Quirrell as *"scared of his own students, scared of his own subject"[8]* provides a much more accurate depiction seeing as his students have to endure awkward introductions, textbook copying and unhelpful lessons on vampire-lizards. If Professor Quirrell was happier with who he was as a person then he would never have sought out the Dark Arts for recognition. He could have confidently shaken Harry's hand, led class discussions without stammering and made a greater impact on his students' lives. As it stands, his two-faced personality gets in the way of his teaching and ultimately leads him down a path of anxiety, mediocrity and a student murder attempt.

PROFESSOR LOCKHART

ATTENTION-SEEKING * INEPT

*"Tut, tut — hardly any of you remembered that my favorite color is
lilac. I say so in Year with the Yeti."* [1]

DEFENSE AGAINST THE DARK ARTS

After a terrible first year in Defense Against the Dark Arts, Harry is
hoping his next professor will make up for all the wasted time listening to
Voldemort's nervous co-teacher. Unfortunately, only one person applies
for the job and he is far from competent. Prior to teaching at Hogwarts,
Gilderoy Lockhart had been famous in the magical community for writing
books such as *Holidays with Hags* and *Voyages with Vampires* where he
portrays himself as the dashing hero. Women across the wizarding world
swoon at his immaculate style and award-winning smile. Even Mrs.
Weasley turns into a blushing fangirl upon meeting him in the bookstore.

But this isn't enough for Lockhart. No, he craves an even more
constant recognition. He decides to become a teacher because, you know,
teaching is so glamorous. Even his announcement of his new position acts

as a publicity stunt. He drags Harry in front of the press, stating students will not just be getting Lockhart's book *Magical Me*, they'll be getting *"the real magical me."²* Professor Lockhart has as much experience teaching as he does tackling dangerous beasts: exactly zero, and it shows during his time at Hogwarts. The reflection off his wardrobe is the brightest thing to happen in his classroom.

✳ ATTENTION-SEEKING ✳

Professor Lockhart is a self-centered, attention-seeking, egotistical manchild. He loves himself more than anyone or anything else. For the most part, there is something to be said about confidence in our abilities, especially in the role of an educator. We have to be the authority figure on all matters and it helps to exude a sense of self-assurance. After Professor Quirrell, confidence should be refreshing, but Gilderoy Lockhart exhibits far too much pride in his abilities.

In their first Defense Against the Dark Arts lesson Lockhart begins by picking up Neville's book which has his winking portrait on the front (that he required all students to purchase) and says *"Me."* His first word to his new class is literally 'me.' Subtle. He goes on to list his achievements including Five-time winner of Witch Weekly's Most-Charming-Smile Award. After this conceited introduction, he has the students take a quiz all about him that takes 30 minutes to complete. Are you kidding me? 30 minutes! I can barely come up with 3 facts about myself for icebreakers but Lockhart has no problem developing a 54 question pop quiz.

Even if it is far more egotistical than it needs to be, this isn't the worst ever start to a class. Most teachers will spend some time on the first day telling students about themselves. I often joke with my students about how awesome I am, overemphasizing it so they know I'm kidding. One of the questions I give my students on the first day of school asks them to list their favorite teacher. I like to tell them "Feel free to put me down as your favorite. I know you have only known me for a full—" I look down at my watch, "—seven minutes, but trust me it will become true soon anyway." Maybe I am channeling a little bit of my inner Lockhart, but it does help lighten the mood.

After the 30 minute quiz Lockhart does attempt what could be a legitimate lesson on Cornish pixies, but he fails miserably and reverts back to his specialty: focusing all the attention on him. From that point on he spends every class period reading from his own books or reenacting his incredible—and entirely fake—achievements. Lockhart attempts to feed off Harry's fame by forcing him to act alongside him by impersonating a villager with a Babbling Curse or a yeti with a head cold. In one particular lesson he makes him hunch over and imitate a werewolf:

> "Nice loud howl, Harry — exactly — and then, if you'll believe it, I pounced — like this — slammed him to the floor — thus — with one hand, I managed to hold him down — with my other, I put my wand to his throat — I then screwed up my remaining strength and performed the immensely complex Homorphus Charm — he let out a piteous groan — go on, Harry — higher than that — good — the fur vanished — the fangs shrank — and he turned back into a man."[3]

After this embarrassing lesson, Lockhart makes the students compose a poem about his defeat of the werewolf. Would they get credit if they wrote about Harry's performance? I'm sure the only criteria Lockhart looks for in his homework are compliments from his fans. I had a teacher who would return work with full marks and no commentary, even when it was written in a different language, clearly not bothering to read a single word. I'm sure Lockhart does this often, but instead of giving an A+ at the top he gets out his flamboyant quill and signs it with his loopy, over-practiced autograph.

The only reason Lockhart should ever tell this story is if his entire lesson is on werewolves. Even then, the story would only be appropriate after providing background knowledge on these creatures. Giving students statistics on the number of werewolves in the world, when they transform and how to protect themselves against attacks is crucial for a Defense Against the Dark Arts class. Telling a personal story to supplement lessons is a great way to get students to remember the content and make real world connections but Lockhart fails to deliver even the basics. Instead, he focuses the whole lesson on his own achievements, never bothering to include any proper instruction. He doesn't even warn students to never approach a werewolf. The only thing students will get out of this lesson is evidence that Lockhart is full of himself (something they knew on day one) and perhaps encouragement to replicate his dangerous feats in search of fame.

Evident in the structure of his lessons, Professor Lockhart will always put himself before the needs of any student. An inexperienced teacher can learn the content and figure out how to manage a class better or make their lessons more engaging, but they can't learn how to love their students. This is a natural ability. For the longest time I thought that I wanted to teach elementary school. That is, until I volunteered in one. Those kids were the whiniest, neediest, dirtiest bunch of tiny humans I had ever seen. My goals changed almost immediately and I gained new respect for elementary school teachers. Working with older students is a much better fit for me. I love their unique personalities and sense of humor. Plus I love being able to tell a student, 'You're bothering me—go away' without making them cry! No bathroom accidents is another major plus. I could have learned to teach younger kids, but I could never learn to love the interactions with those students as much as the insightful discussions I have with my own.

However, a simple change in grade levels wouldn't fix anything for Lockhart. He only teaches for the glory, and this is a terrible reason to become a teacher. Surprisingly, it took me several years to fully learn this lesson. I attended a great high school where as a student I wanted to be as good as everyone else, if not better. When I made the decision to become a teacher and after that terribly noisy day in an elementary school, I was determined to get a job at my alma mater. I pictured myself becoming the next generation's favorite teacher. What better way to prove that I was just as intelligent as those top students than to go back and teach at our high school? I pursued this dream all throughout college until finally I began to coach and student-teach there. Walking those familiar halls with a staff badge made me feel powerful (aside from the day I wore heels to impress the students and fell down a flight of stairs). They didn't have any jobs available yet but when they asked me to wait I felt it was a sign that this was where I was meant to end up.

This was my dream, but seeing as I was wearing the same work pants every day of the week, I clearly needed money. I took a job at one of the lowest achieving junior high schools in town, the complete opposite of where I had envisioned myself. It was a challenging place for a twenty-two-year-old to start her teaching career. I had some of my worst days there, but I fell in love with my students' character and determination to improve despite the circumstances they were born into. I came to realize that teaching wasn't about the accolades, but the difference we can make in individual students' lives. I had been working at this school for two years when I got the call from my old high school about a position. All those feelings came back to me. I could be important. All those people who doubted me along the way would see that I was capable of succeeding at the highest level. After the interview I knew I had to make a decision and quickly. No sane person would turn down this job. I got the call only two hours after the interview offering me the position. The person who called was ecstatic, we had been planning this for years and it was all coming to fruition. As I paced back and forth in my backyard, I made the hardest decision of my life—I turned the job down.

I realized that while the desire for recognition may have pushed me to be more successful in college, it was the students at the low-performing school that had captured my heart. It has been years since that decision and even on my roughest days—and there have been some really *really* rough days (like, Hagrid running into his hut crying rough)—I haven't regretted this decision once. I only regret leaving those teachers at my alma mater behind. They were my inspiration and heroes and I felt I had let them down. But I was no longer getting into this career to gain esteem. Now, the only thing that motivates me day to day is to be better for the students who need me.

Lockhart never learns this lesson. He is so focused on absorbing attention that he neglects the needs and personalities of the students around him. This is best seen in his exploitation of Harry's fame. He forces Harry to take pictures and sign fan mail and pulls him into the spotlight any chance possible, not realizing that what Harry really desires is a quiet, peaceful existence. Harry even begins to hide from Lockhart whenever he's in the vicinity. Lockhart does send Hermione a get-well card when she's in the hospital wing, but I suspect he was just hoping someone would notice and write an article about it for the Daily Prophet. Lockhart fails to make real connections with his students because he's incapable of looking any further than his own reflection in the mirror. Where a good teacher would push their students to accomplish remarkable endeavors for themselves, Lockhart only boasts about his own.

✳ INEPT ✳

If narcissism was Professor Lockhart's only flaw, then he might have still managed to become a decent teacher. It turns out, however, he is so incompetent at the subject matter that Hogwarts must have been extremely desperate for a teacher, because anyone with even the least amount of scrutiny wouldn't hire him.

In his first lesson he attempts to teach the students about Cornish pixies—tiny, blue, devilish creatures that are known to cause as much mischief as possible. Lockhart hides them under a cage and presents these beasts in dramatic fashion:

"It is my job to arm you against the foulest creatures known to wizard-kind! You may find yourselves facing your worst fears in this room. Know only that no harm can befall you whilst I am here. All I ask is that you remain calm."

Despite Ron's disbelief and the rest of the class's laughter at Lockhart's flamboyant introduction, the students still sit up in anticipation of the hidden creatures. Lockhart's enjoyment of the spotlight helps him to create a moment where Harry is actually excited in a Defense Against the Dark Arts classroom for likely the first time. While not much, this is Lockhart's best teaching moment.

He continues with, *"I must ask you not to scream...It might provoke them."* This riveting introduction has the students eager to see what monstrosity he has brought. However, when it turns out to be small, seemingly harmless creatures called Cornish pixies they begin to laugh. While slightly humiliating for Lockhart, it is still possible for him to recover. He could casually brush off their laughter and explain the type of trouble these creatures create or that it is necessary to start small in order to prepare for the real horrors of the world. Instead, out of petty spite he does the worst thing imaginable—releases all of the pixies at once into a classroom full of eleven-year-olds:

> *It was pandemonium. The pixies shot in every direction like rockets. They grabbed ink bottles and sprayed the class with them, shredded books and papers, tore pictures from the walls, up-ended the waste basket, grabbed bags and books and threw them out of the smashed window; within minutes, half the class was sheltering under desks and Neville was swinging from the iron chandelier in the ceiling.* [4]

I have made some bad decisions in my career, like planning a lesson to replicate the feel of an assembly line by having students make paper airplanes—only to realize upon getting to school that September 11th probably isn't the best day for this. A tragic oversight, but at least I've never had a student dangling from the ceiling. This is next level incompetence. But Lockhart could have easily avoided this situation if he had adequately prepared his students. He gives them no directions, somehow expecting students to deal with these demented creatures without any prior knowledge.

Imagine how differently the lesson could have gone if he had prepared the students by telling them which spell to use. He could then take out one Cornish pixie and model the spell for them. After this, the students would practice the spell on their own without any creatures before he finally releases one or two Cornish pixies at a time to practice on as a class. With these small changes this might have been an effective lesson. These creatures do seem to wreak havoc in many places so it would be an important skill for them to learn. Instead, the class is in chaos and the students have lost all respect for Professor Lockhart.

After all these mistakes, it's still possible, believe it or not, for Lockhart to recover the lesson. If he could manage to stop the pixies using a spell similar to the one Hermione later uses to immobilize them, then he could easily prove to the class the necessity of learning how to defend themselves against these monsters now that students have seen it firsthand. But Lockhart panics. The spell he attempts to use doesn't work and the pixies throw his wand out the window. As Neville falls from the chandelier, Lockhart dives under his desk then asks Harry, Ron and Hermione to put the pixies back in their cage while everyone else quickly files out. It takes all of one lesson for Harry and Ron to realize they're in for another year of disappointment. As time goes on and lessons fail to improve, they come to loathe his class and even Lockhart himself.

This isn't Lockhart's only moment of ineptitude. Later in the school year he accidentally removes all Harry's bones from his arm, personally allows students to walk around the corridors without supervision with a monster on the loose, signs a permission slip allowing second years to check out a forbidden book titled *Most Potente Potions*, and even decides to run away when Ginny Weasley's life is in stake. All of these are terrible instances, but one of his worst teaching moments has to be his handling of the dueling club. While teaching students to duel itself might not be the best idea, they were super excited to join and clubs are a good way to help students feel invested and connected to their school. For this purpose it's commendable, just poorly executed.

His first mistake was choosing Professor Snape to be his assistant. Snape hates most people and desperately wants to see Lockhart fail so this is probably the only reason he agreed to help in the first place.

His biggest mistake, however, is handling the club in a very Lockhart-ish manner. He decides to demonstrate dueling first. Many students here from both magical and Muggle homes have never seen a real duel before so this is a good idea. However, the demonstration doesn't end well for Lockhart. As they raise their wands, Snape cries *"Expelliarmus"* and Lockhart flies backward, hits the wall and is left humiliated, sprawled out on the floor:

> *"Well there you have it!" he said, tottering back onto the platform. "That was a Disarming Charm — as you see, I've lost my wand— yes, an excellent idea to show them that, Professor Snape, but if you don't mind my saying so, it was obvious what you were about to do. If I had wanted to stop you it would have been only too easy — however, I felt it would be instructive to let them see..."*

Who starts a dueling club full of young adults and doesn't think of teaching them how to disarm? He clearly just wants to become the popular teacher, but even then this is awful planning. Someone is going to get hurt. Lockhart decides there shouldn't be any more demonstrations, because, you know, watching him fall on his bum was a great way to learn proper dueling skills.

> *"When I count to three, cast your charms to disarm your*
> *opponents — only to disarm them — we don't want any*
> *accidents — one… two … three — "*

Students are split into pairs, some with terrible partnerships like Harry/Draco and Hermione/Millicent Bulstrode from Slytherin. Lockhart tells them to only disarm their partner, but he never even showed them how to disarm! How can he expect them to know it based off of one demonstration Snape gave? The only thing the kids paid attention to was Lockhart making a fool of himself. Students are bleeding, Harry's legs won't stop dancing beneath him and Hermione is in a headlock before Lockhart shouts at them to stop:

> *"I think I better teach you how to block unfriendly spells,"*
> *said Lockhart, standing flustered in the midst of the hall.*

Oh, great idea. I'm sure this will go just as well as his other lessons:

> *"When Draco points his wand at you, you do this."*
> *He raised his own wand, attempted a complicated sort of*
> *wiggling action, and dropped it. Snape smirked as Lockhart*
> *quickly picked it up, saying, "Whoops — my wand is a little*
> *overexcited — "*[5]

Lockhart doesn't end up showing Harry or any of the students how to actually disarm an opponent. He only pretends to show them, skirting around the issue like a politician answering a question. This is extremely important information, especially for Harry who has several duels in his future. However, Lockhart completely fails to teach the students anything at the dueling club aside from proving that Lockhart is once again totally inept at his job and that Harry is a Parselmouth. Why did Dumbledore approve this?

As if this isn't enough to prove that Lockhart is an awful teacher, he is also completely oblivious to what is going on around him. He has no clue how to read people's reactions to his insanity. On his first day at

Hogwarts, he interrupts Professor Sprout and takes Harry out of her class without even really asking her permission. Lockhart doesn't realize he is interrupting real learning when asking to keep Harry from her class, stemming from the fact that he is completely unaware that no learning is occurring in his own classroom. He is so self-involved that I highly doubt he cares if his students are learning at all. Lockhart simply wanted to become more famous, but sadly there are too many teachers in the world who are unaware if their students are learning.

Following Quirrell's skittish teaching style, students came into their second year with high hopes. Instead they are met with a gaudy buffoon who does nothing but talk about himself for an entire year. The only class he might be qualified to teach is drama, and even then he would be a terrible director and just cast himself as the lead role. Both students and staff come to loathe his gregarious personality and teacher-centered methods. Ron questions the value of Defense Against the Dark Arts itself, *"Not the way Lockhart teaches it… I haven't learned anything from him except not to set pixies loose."* And after his memory charm backfires, even Lockhart feels he shouldn't teach, saying: *"Am I a professor? … Goodness, I expect I was hopeless, was I?"*[6] Yes, Lockhart, you were.

PROFESSOR LUPIN

ADVOCATE * EMPATHETIC

"That suggests that what you fear most of all is — fear. Very wise, Harry." [1]

DEFENSE AGAINST THE DARK ARTS

At this point, Harry, Ron and Hermione have had one Defense Against the Dark Arts teacher with Voldemort attached to his head and the other with, well, a big head. It says a lot about their previous two teachers that most students never realized their third professor is a werewolf despite having learned about them both years. Students initially view Professor Lupin as merely the next teacher coming in to fill the void and, understandably given past experience, expect him to be terrible at his job. While Lupin does leave at the end of Harry's third year, he ends up being one of the best teachers Hogwarts has to offer and certainly one of the students' favorites. Only the Slytherins can muster up negative reviews and those are directly related to his old, patched wardrobe—not his lessons. Due to his geniality and practical teaching style, Professor Lupin is not only the first Defense Against the Dark Arts teacher to fill this classroom with learning on a consistent basis, but the best in the subject in all seven years.

✳ ADVOCATE ✳

Imagine the first day of school as a student. You're wearing brand new shoes, seeing old friends again. You walk into class and see a wardrobe rattling suspiciously. What are you thinking? Scared? Excited? This teacher just might be crazy? These thoughts would be justified, but above all you and the other students feel the same way: intrigued.

Professor Lupin begins his first day by telling students to put their books away and get out their wands. Finally, some proper instruction! Prior to this, Professor Lockhart's first day was the closest they've had to a practical lesson and all he did was undo a latch on a cage, releasing pixies into bedlam. Lupin, however, immediately gives the students a sense of purpose by leading them out of the normal Defense Against the Dark Arts classroom—a change of scenery already captivating students—and into the staffroom where a wardrobe has been infested with a boggart (a shape-shifting creature that invades wizard homes). Professor Snape happens to be there and advises Lupin not to give Neville anything difficult. Neville, who had been forced to feed drops of potion to his pet toad in Snape's previous class, now has to tolerate further torment in front of his new teacher. Instead of feeding into Snape's vindictiveness, Professor Lupin tactfully responds *"I was hoping Neville would assist me with the first stage of the operation… and I'm sure he will perform it admirably."*

By standing up for Neville, Lupin quickly dismisses any notion that students will feel inferior in his class and begins to win the trust of students who, like Harry, feel Snape is a bully. He doesn't let students dwell on this awkward interaction (readers later learn these two have a harrowing past) and moves on with the lesson:

"Boggarts like dark, enclosed spaces," said Professor Lupin. "This one moved in yesterday afternoon, and I asked the headmaster if the staff would leave it to give my third years some practice."

Lupin describes places he has seen boggarts like a cabinet under the sink and the inside of a grandfather clock. For the first time, these students get to see a Defense Against the Dark Arts teacher give actual background knowledge before tasking them with practical application. At this point, Lupin gets the class more involved in the discussion and asks them to describe a boggart. Hermione, like countless times before, immediately puts her hand in the air and explains how a boggart will take the shape of a person's greatest fear. Lupin tells Hermione, *"Couldn't have put it better myself,"* causing her to beam. This is especially meaningful to her as she was also on the receiving end of Professor Snape's insults after helping save Neville's toad. With Lupin's confidence in Neville and praise of Hermione, their days improve dramatically after just a few minutes in his presence. Lupin continues his lesson:

"Nobody knows what a boggart looks like when he is alone, but when I let him out, he will immediately become whatever each of us most fears."

"This means," said Professor Lupin, choosing to ignore Neville's small sputter of terror, "that we have a huge advantage over the boggart before we begin. Have you spotted it, Harry?"[2]

Hermione is bouncing up and down ready to give the answer as Lupin directs this next question to Harry. Instead of choosing Hermione's outstretched hand—the quicker option—Professor Lupin draws Harry into the conversation. Getting a feel for what other students are thinking and trusting other students' opinions is essential in leading a class discussion. Every school contains at least one Hermione and it's easy to pick this student as soon as their hand shoots into the air. But doing this allows the Hermiones to dominate the conversation while the rest become complacent. Other students begin to tune out further inquiries if they feel they don't have the chance to respond. In my classroom, I want all students to work through the questions in their mind even if they never get the opportunity to share their response aloud.

To achieve this, I used to write my students' names on a deck of cards (easier to hold than popsicle sticks) and shuffle through them to pick students randomly. While this helped get more students involved, it didn't always bring the most thoughtful comments into the discussion. Most students felt compelled to respond simply for participation points. I also found that the students who wouldn't normally speak up could be just as engaged as the Hermiones. These students who have introverted tendencies or who are prone to nervousness like Neville are often much better at formulating responses after given time to think, write or discuss with a partner before sharing aloud with the class. Because of these differences in student's personalities, I no longer use the name-pulling system and instead try to get students involved in a variety of ways like think-pair-shares, digital discussions or simply giving more time to create a response before calling on students. After directing the question towards Harry, Professor Lupin does exactly this. He pauses and gives Harry time to think before he correctly answers the question. He then directs students' attention to the spell that will get rid of the boggart:

> *"The charm that repels a boggart is simple, yet it requires force of mind. You see, the thing that really finishes a boggart is laughter."*
>
> *"We will practice the charm without wands first. After me, please... riddikulus!*

At last! Unlike Lockhart, Professor Lupin actually models the spell first and has his students practice the charm without wands. After rehearsing, Lupin turns his attention back to Neville and asks for his greatest fear. Neville is so nervous to speak his fear aloud that no noise comes out as he moves his lips. And Lupin cheerfully replies, *"Didn't catch that, Neville, sorry."*[3]

Even after Neville shows obvious signs of fear and incompetence, Professor Lupin still has faith in him. Many teachers, myself included, would choose the student who was guaranteed to perform the best in order to provide an adequate example. Lupin, however, chooses the least successful student who has no self-confidence! He responds to Neville's terror with a calm and amusing demeanor helping to counteract some of the fear he is exuding. Still looking for reassurance from the class, Neville cautiously whispers Professor Snape's name causing everyone to laugh, and a smile to break through his usual nervous composure. This might be the first time—outside Herbology—that Neville has actually smiled in a class setting. It's Professor Lupin's refreshing approach to the lesson that helps Neville feel comfortable enough to laugh. Lupin moves on, asking Neville a few questions about his grandmother's clothes and then explains his expectations:

> *"When the boggart bursts out of this wardrobe, Neville, and sees you, it will assume the form of Professor Snape," said Lupin. "And you will raise your wand — thus — and cry 'Riddikulus' — and concentrate hard on your grandmother's clothes."*
>
> *"If Neville is successful, the boggart is likely to shift his attention to each of us in turn," said Professor Lupin. "I would like all of you to take a moment now to think of the thing that scares you most, and imagine how you might force it to look comical...."*[4]

By using Neville's fear as an example, the class knows exactly what is expected of them when it's their turn to face the boggart. Lupin gives students time to think through their greatest fear and how to transform it into something humorous. Harry takes longer than others (never fully landing on a fear) but the rest of the class is focused and ready by the time Professor Lupin begins to count. As he hits the number three, out walks Professor Boggart Snape. Neville hesitates and mumbles through the charm, but he manages to change the boggart's attire into his grandmother's. The class roars with laughter as Neville steps back for someone else's turn in the spotlight. Neville was only able to get this moment of triumph because Professor Lupin was willing to test his abilities. Several others are given a chance with the boggart, laughter constantly filling the room, before Lupin gives Neville a final crack at the creature. Grandma Snape returns and this time Neville approaches it with renewed strength and determination. He shouts the spell and lets out a burst of laughter that leads to the boggart's death.

Lupin's faith in Neville helped his confidence grow tremendously within just a short time span. He went from being terrified of Snape and the boggart, muttering his charm barely loud enough for others to hear, to charging at the creature with assurance. Throughout the series we watch Neville progress from a timid first year to a hero. It is with Lupin's guidance (along with Professor Sprout's) that he begins the journey towards snake-killing champion of Gryffindor.

In the Muggle world we don't often get to witness our students turn into sword carrying heroes. Unless they seek me out—or I awkwardly run into them at the grocery store buying beer—I usually won't know what type of person they grew into. One day I was sitting at my desk planning lessons, seriously contemplating giving up and assigning bookwork. I was tired of spending hours creating interactive lessons just to have my students sit there. What did it matter? Sometimes it seemed like they were all turning into little Death Eaters anyway. As I was pondering this a former student walked in. From the moment she stepped over the threshold the maturity in her was apparent. She apologized for the way she used to act in my class (I distinctly remember her telling me to 'F— off' on several occasions) and wanted to thank me for not giving up on her. She didn't turn to the Dark Arts! Yay!

She pointed to a half finished assignment on the Gettysburg Address lying on my desk and mentioned that engaging lessons like that were what helped keep her focused in school. Hoping she didn't have Snape's ability to read minds, and now feeling extremely guilty, I talked to her for fifteen more minutes about her future plans. After she left, I closed the textbook and finished the other half of the assignment where students would be turning Lincoln's Speech into tweets. Her words of appreciation, while small, were the reminder I needed that even if we don't see the progress, the work we put in for our students does impact them.

Professor Lupin never gets to see the effects of his teaching beyond the Battle of Hogwarts, but this never hinders his motivation. After Lupin's amusing lesson, he assigns homework where they are tasked with summarizing the chapter on boggarts—not nearly as fun as defending themselves against the boggart itself, but a huge improvement over composing poems about Lockhart. And now they have practical experience to back up their informative writing.

Lupin's first lesson with his third years has been a huge success. He helped turn Hermione's mood around, built up Neville's confidence and had the class laughing and engaged the entire period. As an informal way of getting to know each other they also learned their classmates' greatest fears and sense of humor. This is a great start to the year and the students quickly fall in love with Lupin's class.

On the first day of school I try to gain this type of engagement by using a strategy I learned from a former professor called Artifact Collection. As students walk into my classroom they see several brown paper bags lined against the wall. I lead them through a discussion on the meaning of the word artifact, trying to draw others into the conversation like Lupin does with Harry. Many will say an artifact is something old, using bones as their go-to example. I guide them to the meaning I want them to gain: an artifact is an object from history that tells us how people lived. It usually takes a few minutes for students to feel comfortable with talking on the first day, but kids are generally ready to be heard as long as I'm willing to listen.

Once everyone understands my definition, I explain that these bags hold my personal artifacts. Instead of spending our first hour together recounting my (rather boring) life story, they look through my artifacts and try to determine my likes and dislikes. As a group they touch, examine, and draw conclusions based on the objects and then share their findings with the rest of the class. One bag could include a red and yellow knit scarf, a recent plane ticket, a jar of peanut butter, my college soccer jersey, or a picture of my dog. While this activity sounds more like Lockhart's self-centered quiz than Lupin's wardrobe activity, it forces me to reveal much more about myself than I would normally feel comfortable sharing. Students get to spend more time talking with each other than listening to me and in the process know that I am entrusting them with some of my most valuable possessions. This helps to make students comfortable in my classroom and sets a tone of mutual respect for the rest of the year, just as Lupin has done with his lesson on boggarts. From here on out both sets of students come into class excited and ready to learn. They are confident that we have faith in them and are much more willing to listen because of it.

We see Professor Lupin advocate for students other times throughout the series. In Harry's third year Professor Snape catches him with the Marauder's Map. Snape has a suspicion about the old parchment and calls Lupin in for a second opinion. While Snape is trying to punish Harry, claiming the map is full of dark magic, Lupin scoffs at this idea and tries to convince Snape it must be a joke shop item. As one of the creators, Lupin knows all too well that the parchment is an enchanted map of Hogwarts (his nickname is on the front after all). He could have sided with his colleague but knows that leaving Snape to discipline Harry will do more harm than good:

"Don't expect me to cover up for you again, Harry. I cannot make you take Sirius Black seriously.... Your parents gave their lives to keep you alive, Harry. A poor way to repay them — gambling their sacrifice for a bag of magic tricks."[5]

Snape attempted to ridicule Harry into submission, but Lupin takes a different approach—with greater effect. Harry feels much worse after one calm discussion with Lupin than any moment with Snape. Lupin knows that reasoning with Harry is the only method of persuasion that will work. While lying to another teacher is obviously frowned upon, his actions keep his student safe both from Snape's malice and Harry's own reckless desires to confront a murderer.

However, even with these run-ins and latent school animosity, Lupin still advocates for Snape. Although this bothers Harry, Lupin dismisses any notions that Snape shouldn't be trusted. Lupin's willingness to advocate for those around him is an admirable quality. Whether tormented student or misunderstood staff, Professor Lupin always speaks up for what is right.

✳ EMPATHETIC ✳

Professor Lupin has an affable quality about him that makes him one of the most welcoming teachers at Hogwarts. I've only met a few people who have a certain intimate presence. When I'm around them, I feel 100% at ease. This is a strange sensation for me since I feel uncomfortable in many situations. But when I'm with these people, personal information slips unwillingly past the protective spells of my mind and out into the open. Like Lockhart's pixies, my deep-seated thoughts spew out, bumping into each other, causing trouble and not making much sense outside the confines of my mind. My confidant sits there taking it all in and is, somehow, able to immobilize the thoughts and organize them into meaning. I leave their presence feeling slightly more understood but also like a bludger has just struck me in the gut for sharing more information than I wanted. Professor Lupin has this same effect on people. If I were his colleague or student, I fear I would share way too many personal feelings over a cup of tea in his office. It's this personality trait, though, that makes students feel comfortable enough to approach him about all matters, seeking advice even outside the classroom.

Harry, not allowed into Hogsmeade, runs into Lupin while wandering around the castle by himself. Lupin invites him in for a cup of tea, already making him a much better person than I am, because—as much as I love them—sometimes I just want students to go away. He pulls out a kettle and taps it with his wand, instantly making the water hot. Maybe I'd invite more students in for tea if I didn't have to wait two minutes for my microwave to heat up the water. As they're talking, Lupin notices that something is bothering Harry and asks what is wrong. Harry questions Lupin about his interference with the boggart. He feels Lupin deliberately didn't let Harry face the creature. Lupin, surprised by this line of questioning, tells Harry he thought the boggart would turn into Lord Voldemort as soon as it landed at Harry's feet. Could you imagine?! Lord Volde-ggart strutting around the staffroom would be a terrible idea! Smart move by Lupin. He asks Harry, *"So you've been thinking that I didn't believe you capable of fighting the boggart?"* [6]

This has been bothering Harry for several chapters and may have stayed with him forever, hindering his ability to learn proper defensive spells. Even after believing his professor thinks he's incapable, Harry still feels comfortable enough to question him. Lupin's main concern is not that Harry is questioning his decisions as a professor, but rather, that his student thought he didn't believe in him. This speaks to the empathy and love Lupin has for his students. We can't all have this naturally welcoming personality, but his attitude towards his students is something we can strive to emulate. I have a resting face that closely resembles Madam Pince when a student asks her to use the restricted section, so it's something I have to be conscious of, especially at the end of the day when I'm most exhausted.

Although not clearly pointed out in the book, this interaction between Harry and Lupin takes place on Halloween, the anniversary of Lily and James's deaths. Harry doesn't give the date much thought—he's mostly depressed about not visiting Hogsmeade—but I'm sure Professor Lupin remembers. They were his best friends after all. His willingness to give up some of his time to comfort Harry is amazingly thoughtful.

✳ ✳ ✳

Harry falls off his broom later in the school year as a dementor flies over his Quidditch match, causing him to become exceedingly insecure about his inability to combat these spooky creatures. It doesn't help that Malfoy teases him endlessly about it. After a great lesson on hinkypunks, Lupin asks Harry to stay behind to offer his condolences on his destroyed broomstick. Harry timidly brings up the incident with the dementors and asks Lupin, *"Why do they affect me like that? Am I just —"* Lupin cuts Harry off before he can spit the words out. *"It has nothing to do with weakness,"* *said Professor Lupin sharply, as though he had read Harry's mind.* [7]

After Lupin says this, the room literally brightens as he helps Harry overcome his insecurities. Lupin goes on to explain why he shouldn't feel ashamed, explaining that the dementors have a greater effect on people who have had greater horrors in their past.

Lupin initiates this conversation knowing that the Quidditch match was having a detrimental effect on Harry. This creates a safe environment where Harry feels comfortable enough to share his fears. He even goes on to tell Lupin that when he faces dementors he hears his mother being murdered by Voldemort, something he hasn't shared with anyone before. At the end of this conversation Lupin offers to show Harry how to defend himself against dementor attacks.

The first of these anti-dementor lessons takes place after Christmas. Professor Lupin teaches Harry about Patronuses and has him practice the incantation a few times without the boggart (acting as a pretend dementor) present. When Harry passes out on his first real attempt, Lupin simply hands him chocolate and reassures him saying, *"I didn't expect you to do it your first time; in fact, I would have been astounded if you had."*[8]

After his second attempt, Harry passes out for a longer amount of time and now hears his dad fighting off Voldemort. Lupin begins to have second thoughts. If Harry is hearing both his parents being murdered repeatedly, then maybe he has been pushing him too hard. Not to mention it must be difficult for Lupin to relive the memory of their deaths as well. Harry is adamant that they continue and Lupin gives him one more shot at it. On his third attempt Harry manages to hold off the dementor for a short amount of time before Lupin forces it back into the case while giving Harry high praise. Later sessions are not as successful but Lupin never gives up hope on Harry:

> *"You're expecting too much of yourself...For a thirteen-year-old wizard, even an indistinct Patronus is a huge achievement."*
>
> ...
>
> *"If the dementor put in an appearance at your next Quidditch match, you will be able to keep them at bay long enough to get back to the ground."*
>
> ...
>
> *"I have complete confidence in you,"* said Lupin, smiling.

After bolstering Harry's confidence, they have a deep discussion about the dementor's kiss and whether anyone deserves to have their soul sucked out. Harry has been contemplating revenge against Sirius Black for the betrayal that (he believes) led to his parents' deaths, so this discussion is a vital moment in Harry's moral development. Lupin asks: *"Do you really think anyone deserves that?"*[9] Although Harry's initial response is yes, at the end of the year he spares Peter Pettigrew's life (the actual betrayer) suggesting his opinion has changed. In Harry's world—and arguably ours—killing has metaphysical consequences. His reluctance to kill becomes a trademark of Harry's throughout the rest of the series and a steadfast demonstration of his heroic strength.

Professor Lupin's willingness to spend extra hours helping Harry learn the Patronus charm leads to this defining ethical discussion. While we can't all take as much time as Lupin after hours to help our students (he does live on the campus after all), we can learn from his willingness to have open discussions with them. Such a simple act as keeping Harry after class to ask how he was doing after the Quidditch match is something we can all model in our classrooms.

Unlike the majority of the professors we read about throughout the series, Professor Lupin provides a genuinely welcoming presence. Students feel comfortable enough to approach him after school hours for help and advice. We mainly see this in Harry's interactions with Professor Lupin, but I would bet that he would react the same way if it was Ernie McMillan, Luna Lovegood or even Draco Malfoy. I can't imagine Lupin limiting his kindness simply to those of Gryffindor house.

* * *

Professor Lupin is not only extremely kind, but also immensely cool in the eyes of his teenage students. Harry's first interaction with Professor Lupin wasn't in the classroom, but on the train ride to Hogwarts. A dementor had just boarded their train causing Harry to momentarily pass out. Lupin shielded the students and quickly passed around chocolate for them to eat. An act that makes Madam Pomfrey exclaim, *"We've finally got a defense Against the Dark Arts teacher who knows his remedies."* When Harry doesn't immediately eat the chocolate Lupin comments, *"I haven't poisoned that chocolate, you know..."*[10] It's such a small, sarcastic comment that could get overlooked, but this mollifies Harry enough to eat, helping him feel better immediately. Lupin's lighthearted humor is much more effective in this instance than any stern insistence.

On their way to the staffroom on the first day they come across Peeves sticking gum in a keyhole and all eyes turn towards Lupin to see how he will react. His students are shocked to see him smiling when he tells Peeves to remove the gum. When Peeves ignores this demand, Lupin pulls out his wand, telling his class to pay attention as he points it at the poltergeist. The gum shoots out of the keyhole and right into Peeve's nose as he flies away, leaving the class amazed. In the eyes of Lupin's students, he stood up to Peeves in the coolest way possible. He didn't call for Dumbledore or simply ignore him. No, he actually shot the gum back at Peeves!

Flinging gum at someone isn't the only way to relate to students while maintaining authority—our best relationships form out of our personalities. Depending on how we present ourselves to the class, each of us will make better connections with some students over others. Professor Sprout connects with Neville over their mutual adoration of plants, while Flitwick makes a better connection with Hermione out of her love of knowledge.

Even my TV watching habits have helped make connections with students I hadn't previously believed possible. In my mid 20's I had a slight obsession with Doctor Who, and when I say slight, I mean all-encompassing. Watching every episode in a few weeks, painting TARDIS shoes, and decorating my home with iconic images from the show. One day while I was preparing a lesson on the Roman Empire, Doctor Who was on in the background and I came up with a brilliant idea. Students would pretend they had traveled through time from that era and write down their reactions to what they see around them. As I created the handout I included the blue police box in the corner as a special touch. The next day as I passed out the activity, I heard Olivia, my shy seventh grade girl, speak up in class for the first time: "Ms. Dickie, do you watch Doctor Who?" It was the loudest I had ever heard her speak and her excitement surprised her as well. After class we had a good discussion about the history in the show and throughout that year we continued to bond over the Doctor and his travels. If I wasn't willing to share my geekiness with my class, I don't think I would have ever made this connection with Olivia. She would have just been another number in the sea of students.

As a werewolf, Professor Lupin is unique among the Hogwarts staff. In the wizarding world, werewolves are viewed as social outcasts in society. J.K. Rowling uses Lupin as an analogy for people afflicted by diseases and who are viewed as inferior or different. It is important for us to remember that our students come in all shapes, colors, and sizes. Yet, the diversity of the teaching staff often does not reflect this widespread diversity that we see sitting in our classrooms. It is extremely important that our students learn from people who have gone through a variety of life experiences that are similar and dissimilar to their own. Lupin's experiences and feelings of insecurities surrounding his condition help him connect with students who are often seen as outcasts in the wizarding world such as Neville, Hermione and Harry. While other teachers might not be able to make this specific connection, they can connect with students in other ways personal to them.

Professor Lupin is a well-rounded teacher who advocates for all students, has a welcoming heart and an ability to connect with his students on a deeper level. His lessons are always well-planned and practical. In his class, students learn how to defend themselves against a wide range of dark creatures including boggarts, hinkypunks, grindylows, and kappas. And at the end of the year, Lupin sets up an obstacle course where students demonstrate their skills facing each of these previously studied beasts that manages to be both comprehensive and fun.

Even several years after his teaching career had ended Lupin still has his students' best interests in mind. In *Deathly Hallows*, while Harry, Ron and Hermione are in hiding and Lupin finds them, Harry demands proof before allowing him to enter. Lupin—using this moment to teach— comments, "*Speaking as your ex-Defense Against the Darks Arts teacher, I quite agree that you had to check. Ron, Hermione, you shouldn't be quite so quick to lower your defenses."*[11] To Lupin, teaching is an opportunity to shape lives. In Harry's words, Lupin is *"the best Defense Against the Dark Arts teacher"*[12] they've ever had, and at the end of the year, even after learning he is a werewolf, the students—and myself—are sad to see him go.

PROFESSOR MOODY

DEMANDING * FORMIDABLE

"That's what I've got to teach you to fight. You need preparing. You need arming. But most of all, you need to practice constant, never-ceasing vigilance."[1]

DEFENSE AGAINST THE DARK ARTS

Harry's fourth Defense Against the Dark Arts professor isn't a vampire, as some students had hoped. Instead, the teacher they get is perhaps even more terrifying. His severe expression, chipped nose, and twisting magical eye are a shocking contrast to Professor Lupin's kind demeanor. Students both young and old are frightened when his entrance—conveniently paired with a lightning storm—interrupts Professor Dumbledore's welcome speech. Taking on the position as a favor to Dumbledore, Alastor 'Mad-Eye' Moody comes back to Hogwarts as a retired Auror and hero of the first wizarding war. His unrelenting form of classroom management and demanding teaching style lead to success in the classroom.

At the end of *Goblet of Fire*, we find out that Professor Moody is actually Barty Crouch Jr., a Death Eater and Lord Voldemort's most loyal servant. He has taken on the real Moody's appearance using Polyjuice Potion in an attempt to lead Harry Potter to his death. Although we never see the real Moody in the classroom, I will continue to use his name throughout this chapter so I don't confuse myself. Considering that Harry's fourth Defense Against the Dark Arts professor is a Death Eater with little obligation to teach well, it makes his accomplishments as a teacher even more impressive.

✳ DEMANDING ✳

Professor Moody begins class unlike any teacher before him. Quirrell had a nervous encounter with Harry, Lockhart made the students take a quiz on his attributes and Lupin had them laughing while learning how to dispel a boggart. Moody, however, decides to skip any formalities and get straight to the lesson:

> "Curses. They come in many strengths and forms. Now, according to the Ministry of Magic, I'm supposed to teach you countercurses and leave it at that. I'm not supposed to show you what illegal Dark curses look like until you're in the sixth year. But... I say, the sooner you know what you're up against, the better. How are you supposed to defend yourself against something you've never seen?"

Diving straight into the material is a good tactic for Moody. Can you imagine him leading icebreaker activities on the first day? I also appreciate his willingness to ignore Ministry suggestion for what he thinks is best for his students. While I would never directly disobey administrators, I often look at the standards in the same manner as Professor Moody—as guidelines. California's standards for U.S. History—a relatively short time frame in comparison to other country's—has eleven main standards and seventy-two sub-standards. The majority of those seventy-two sub-standards can be narrowed down even further. This doesn't even take into account the skill-based standards we are required to cover. Ultimately, it is up to us to determine what is best for our students.

While Moody continues his discussion, Lavender ignores the lesson and shows Parvati her horoscope underneath the table. Moody spots this immediately and shouts *"You need to put that away, Miss Brown, when I'm talking."*[2] Even though Moody doesn't take time to go over any guidelines, pointing out little nuisances effectively takes the place of any long discussion of rules. Now students know: not only can he see through desks, he won't tolerate any distractions in his class.

Even after this intimidating display of authority, several hands raise when Moody asks which curses the Ministry punishes the hardest. Along with Hermione, Ron raises his hand to participate—an uncommon occurrence in any class. He suggests the Imperius Curse to which Moody takes out a spider to demonstrate the curse's effects. As the spider flips, spins and dances the class begins to laugh. Moody addresses the class: *"Think it's funny do you? You'd like it, would you, if I did it to you."*[3] They stop laughing immediately. This seems harsh, but it's important that his students understand the immeasurable amounts of damage this curse has caused.

Professor Moody then directs the class to the next Unforgivable Curse. This time Neville raises his hand to provide a response, surprising Harry and even Neville himself. Moody enlarges the spider so students can adequately see the effect of the Cruciatus Curse, the spell Neville supplies. As Moody cries, *"Crucio,"* the spider writhes in pain across the tabletop causing Neville great distress. Moody—knowing Neville's parents were tortured by the Cruciatus Curse—understands his reaction, but feels this demonstration is too important to skip.

Only the Killing Curse is left for Moody to demonstrate, another spell that has greatly impacted the life of a student in the room. Harry is uneasy as he watches Moody perform Avada Kedavra upon the unknowing spider.

Even Ron—who hasn't experienced loss at the hands of this curse—jumps backwards in shock.

Moody points all attention towards Harry as the only known survivor of the Killing Curse. Harry tries to maintain composure, but can only stare at the blackboard, thinking *"So that was how his parents had died... exactly like that spider.... Had they simply seen the flash of green light and heard the rush of speeding death, before life was wiped from their bodies?"* It takes all of Harry's concentration to draw his attention back to Moody's lesson. Perhaps it would have been sensible to prepare Harry and Neville for what they would undergo in class. Both have been mentally drawn out of the lesson. While this activity is important, their emotional well-being is just as important.

Moody seems to sense their discomfort so he continues with an explanation:

> *"Avada Kedavra's a curse that needs a powerful bit of magic behind it — you could all get your wands out now and point them at me and say the word, and I doubt I'd get so much as a nosebleed. But that doesn't matter, I'm not here to teach you how to do it.*
>
> *"Now, if there's no counter curse, why am I showing you? Because you've got to know. You don't want to find yourself in a situation where you're facing it.*[4]

It's important for students to understand why these curses are unforgivable. Many of Harry's classmates are quickly coming up on their fifteenth birthdays. The Ministry suggests they wait two more years, but Moody is correct in insisting they need to be prepared. Harry in particular needs to understand—Voldemort aims all three Unforgivable Curses at him later this year, after all.

At the age of fourteen in my Muggle school, we were required to take a health class that spent a significant amount of time showing us the effects of the Unforgivable Curses of the real world: sexually transmitted diseases.

As grotesque images of herpes flashed on the projector, the phrase 'and then you will die' seemed to be said more than was necessary outside of a Mean Girls reference. While these pictures were jarring for a sheltered fourteen-year-old girl, these were real dangers students could face and were perhaps necessary to see.

My health teacher also thought it was important we understood the way alcohol impairs our judgement. Rather than simply projecting nauseating images, he had us put on beer goggles and attempt to walk in a straight line. As we clattered through tables and chairs, the more we realized that attempting to drive in this state would be fatal.

Likewise, Professor Moody transitions his lessons to more interactive activities. Instead of showing them vicious curses, he begins casting the Imperius Curse upon each of them. He calls the students forward one by one, each of them unable to throw off the curse. On Harry's first attempt he bangs his shin as he resists Moody's magical demand to jump on the table. After watching students do nothing but yield, Moody's excitement is obvious:

> "Look at that, you lot… Potter fought! He fought it, and he damn near beat it! We'll try that again, Potter, and the rest of you, pay attention — watch his eyes, that's where you see it — very good, Potter, very good indeed! They'll have trouble controlling you!"[5]

He places the curse upon Harry four more times until he's able to completely evade the attack. Moody doesn't give clear instruction on how to resist. Instead, he chooses to use Harry as an example. As the resistance requires strength of mind rather than a specific spell, this proves effective. Now that students have watched Harry's focused determination, they can know exactly what is expected of them the next time they're in the spotlight.

Moody's demanding approach to the subject matter keeps students interested and prepared for the reality of facing the Dark Arts. Even students like Fred, George and Lee Jordan—who usually hate school—find themselves excited to attend Defense Against the Dark Arts lessons. For perhaps the first time in their lives, they exclaim about a professor, *"How cool is he?...He knows, man....Knows what it's like to be out there doing it....He's seen it all."*[6]

❋ FORMIDABLE ❋

Professor Moody's demanding teaching style stems from his intense personality. One of his first acts as a teacher is to turn a student of his into a ferret (it's Draco Malfoy, though, so most are thrilled). Moody shouts, *"OH NO YOU DON'T, LADDIE! I don't like people who attack when their opponent's back's turned. Stinking, cowardly, scummy thing to do...."*[7] When Professor McGonagall sees Moody forcing the ferret-Malfoy to bounce up and down and frantically asks what he was doing. Moody simply replies, *"Teaching."*[8]

Technically, Moody does teach Malfoy something. He learns to fear humiliation while in Moody's presence. This style of discipline might work when training Aurors, but it will not work in a school setting. Malfoy and his friends are certainly hesitant as they enter Defense Against the Dark Arts for the first time, but they also lose respect for Moody. When they need help he will be the last they turn to.

When I reached fifth grade I was placed with my first male teacher, Mr. Feramisco. He looked like an unhappy version of Mr. Clean. The whole first week of school I really thought he hated children. His favorite phrase, 'Sit on your conjunction!' served as an academic way of yelling at students to sit on their ass. Forget your name on an assignment and be prepared for his wrath. A few students even complained and were moved to another class. After a week of torture and a few less students, however, his demeanor changed. While still extremely strict, he also became witty and caring.

Even through his formidable presence, Mr. Feramisco found a way to connect with each of his students. He would spend every recess playing sports with us. Now that I'm a teacher, I appreciate just how much effort this must have taken. He taught us the proper rules of four square ("None of this chicken-legs business") and kids would line up the length of a basketball court for the chance to beat Mr. Feramisco. He would also take whoever was chosen as student of the month out to lunch. And when another teacher thought I gave her attitude (I was just trying to get a drink of water) he believed my account of the story, knowing I would never disobey another adult. He was the first public teacher to influence me, and his challenging teaching style pushed me further than I thought was possible.

Moody, his appearance more unnerving than Mr. Feramisco's, may not play four square in the Hogwarts courtyard, but he still manages to develop relationships with each of his students. After Moody's unsettling demonstration of the Unforgivable Curses, many of the students leave class excitedly talking about the lesson as if it was all a big show, but Harry and Neville are not convinced. Instead, they feel despondent.

Neville merely stands off to the side of the hallway, staring at the wall when Harry, Ron and Hermione approach. They ask if he is okay and he replies, *"Oh yes, I'm fine... Very interesting dinner — I mean lesson — what's for eating?"* Noticing something is clearly wrong, they prepare to ask again when Moody clumps up to them. *"It's alright, sonny,"* he said to Neville. *"Why don't you come up to my office? Come on... we can have a cup of tea...."* Before Moody leaves, he also checks on Harry who is not as visibly upset.

When Harry runs into Neville later that day, he sees he is untroubled and holding a copy of *Magical Water Plants of the Mediterranean* that Professor Moody gave him, saying, *"Apparently, Professor Sprout told Professor Moody I'm really good at Herbology."* Usually the center of every joke, Neville rarely ever gets told he is good at something. Harry feels this is a *"tactful"*[9] way of cheering him up, comparing it to the type of thing Professor Lupin would do. This is high praise from Harry considering

Lupin is his favorite teacher.

Professor Moody demonstrates his understanding of students again when helping Harry prior to the first task of the Triwizard Tournament. As the youngest contestant, Harry feels overwhelmed and insecure about his ability to compete. Moody makes Harry comfortable enough in his presence to admit he feels he has no strengths to draw from:

> "Excuse me," growled Moody, "you've got strengths if I say you've got them. Think now. What are you best at?"
>
> "Quidditch," he said dully, "and a fat lot of help — "
>
> "That's right…You're a damn good flier from what I've heard."
>
> "Yeah, but…" Harry stared at him. "I'm not allowed a broom, I've got my wand — "[10]

With a little encouragement, Moody is able to guide him to the answer and force Harry to think on his own that all he had to do was summon his broom. This is a skill that is essential for his survival not only in the Triwizard Tournament, but also in his many encounters with Voldemort to come. While he may have ulterior motives, Professor Moody's awareness of Neville's distress and Harry's insecurities combined with his ability to snap them out of it are marks of an excellent teacher.

Perhaps the greatest thing Moody does, however, is instill Harry's desire to become an Auror. Prior to speaking with Moody, Harry had hardly thought about what types of jobs are available to wizards. After Harry makes a connection between recent strange events and the Dark Mark at the Quidditch World Cup, Professor Moody tells him: "You ever thought of a career as an Auror…You want to consider it"[11]—high praise from a former Auror.

By the time Moody gives him career advice, Harry has had an eventful evening: a run-in with Snape, a luxurious bath in the off-limits prefects' bathroom, and a chance encounter that leads him to finally figure out the meaning of his Triwizard egg—something that has been nagging at him for months. But these are not at the top of his mind when he clambers into bed later. No, all he can think about is Moody's recommendation. His assurance that Harry would make a great Auror is all Harry needs at this time to set his goals in place. Even after discovering that Professor Moody is an impostor, Harry still determinedly follows this path and begins to take the classes necessary to reach this esteemed profession.

Giving students small reassurances like this is often overlooked. I had the most amazing student my first year of teaching—she was brilliant, athletic, and caring. Everything I could want from a thirteen-year-old student. One day I told her: "You keep this up and you could receive a lot of money for college." Her response shocked me. I assumed she would respond with "I know" or "Cool." But instead she asked, "Really?" Standing before me was a talented young woman and no one had ever told her she could go to college. She had no idea! Her parents didn't know or care. And more surprisingly, no teachers had told her this either. Granted, she was only in junior high, but this is when students need to dream and set goals for their futures.

Even though his appearance is alarming, Professor Moody does a tremendous job helping students overcome their insecurities and preparing them for the horrors they will face in the real world. These skills are extremely necessary in self-protection, especially as Voldemort gains power. His unrelenting form of classroom management and demanding teaching style lead to great success in his class.

But Professor Moody is an imposter and we don't get to see the lasting effects this has on students. They may feel betrayed or confused and question the influence he has had on their lives. In the Muggle world, it is the unfortunate reality that sometimes teachers commit crimes. This can negatively impact students and reshape the way they remember their time together. We don't see much of these lasting impacts at Hogwarts, but it's worth considering that many of Moody's students would feel similar losses. With a slight shift in circumstances, he could have been remembered as one of Harry's best professors.

Imagine if someone had influenced Barty Crouch Jr.—their real professor—as a student and had encouraged him to become a teacher. Maybe he wouldn't have joined the Death Eaters and instead put his efforts towards joining the full-time teaching staff at Hogwarts. Whether for show or out of pride in the job he was fulfilling, Barty Crouch Jr. demands excellence from his students. If we take into account that Harry's fourth Defense Against the Dark Arts professor is actually a Death Eater in disguise it makes his accomplishments as a teacher even more magical. In response to Umbridge displaying disgust that Moody performed illegal spells on students, Dean Thomas said, *"Well, he turned out to be a maniac, didn't he? …Mind you, we still learned loads."*[12] Professor Moody shows us that no matter our background, everyone has the potential to become an excellent teacher.

PROFESSOR UMBRIDGE

Controlling * Malicious

"We will be following a carefully structured, theory-centered, Ministry-approved course of defensive magic this year. Copy down the following, please." [1]

Defense Against the Dark Arts

Dolores Umbridge is described as having a *"toadlike face"* and looking *"like somebody's maiden aunt."* [2] At a time when the Ministry of Magic is actively suppressing the news of Voldemort's return, they appoint Umbridge as the fifth Defense Against the Dark Arts teacher as a means to gain more influence at Hogwarts. At a glance she appears harmless, but it only takes a few words to see how deftly she can manipulate and suppress. When she desires even more power, she is promoted to High Inquisitor (perhaps a role she created herself). This gives her the authority to do what she truly loves—tormenting students and staff. Her resentful and impractical teaching style causes students, staff and fans to loathe her and her fluffy pink cardigan even more than the most evil wizard of all time. Out of all the previous Defense Against the Dark Arts teachers, including two who aligned themselves with Lord Voldemort, Professor Umbridge is by far the worst.

Professor Umbridge's malevolence feels so real because she embodies the very real fears we have experienced with those in a position of authority. All our worst teachers' traits combined into one toadlike woman. We have felt her. Seen her. Experienced her. I have never had a dark wizard out to kill me, but I have survived teachers like Professor Umbridge. Her overfamiliar catty remarks and vicious punishments are nothing but detrimental to the learning environment.

∗ CONTROLLING ∗

Professor Umbridge wastes no time informing the school of her and the Ministry's educational philosophy. She interrupts Dumbledore's opening speech to address the school: *"The treasure trove of magical knowledge amassed by our ancestors must be guarded, replenished, and polished by those who have been called to the noble profession of teaching."* Does this witch really believe she is called to teach?

She continues, *"Progress for progress's sake must be discouraged, for our tried and tested traditions often require no tinkering."*[3] Clearly she hasn't been around education long enough to realize that almost every minute of the school day requires tinkering. We never reach a point where our lessons are perfect. Everything can always be improved.

By the end of her tedious speech, Hermione is the only student paying attention and she translates for Harry and Ron that the Ministry will be interfering at Hogwarts. Umbridge has been here all of one day and already feels she knows better than the rest of the staff.

On the first day of class Professor Umbridge immediately imposes her new ideas upon her students. She forces a mechanical greeting out of them, then demands everyone put their wands away. You might as well tell students in a computer class to put their laptops away and pull out a pencil.

Students are then instructed to copy down her three course aims which are carefully structured to avoid any mention of practicing spells.

Realizing this lesson is getting less interesting by the minute, students merely grumble in reply to her asking if they brought their books. Professor Umbridge, with a barely restrained desire to control all aspects of life at Hogwarts, slowly tells them: *"When I ask you a question, I should like you to reply 'Yes, Professor Umbridge,' or 'No, Professor Umbridge.'"*[4] Making students reply in robotic tones is not a problem itself, but turning students into robots is. Clearly not wanting her students to do any thinking of their own, she then tells them to silently read chapter one.

And that is her entire plan for their first day together. I imagine her lesson plan is written on pink cat stationary that has three objectives for the day: 1) Wands away 2) Copy goals 3) Shut up and read. Worse than any of the previous teachers' first days, she fails to introduce herself and doesn't care to get to know her students.

It only takes a few moments of reading before Umbridge loses her class's focus. Harry's reading the same line over and over while Ron concentrates on twirling his quill. Surprisingly, Hermione isn't reading either. Clearly more entertaining than chapter one, the rest of the class's attention shifts towards Hermione who has her hand in the air. It takes Umbridge several minutes and the distraction of over half the class before she addresses Hermione.

Hermione questions the terminology of the objectives and asks *"Surely the whole point of Defense Against the Dark Arts is to practice defensive spells?"* To attempt to be fair to Umbridge, while Hermione's last two professors taught practical applications of these skills, her first two did not. Perhaps the subject really is meant to be theoretical. However, this is a clever question, and one we should want all our students asking. 'Why is this important?' is usually uttered due to frustration, but it is a legitimate question and something all teachers should be able to answer. I want my students to think critically even if it means questioning me.

In my third year of teaching I had the most inquisitive bunch of twelve-year-olds that I have ever met. They had a hard time understanding chronology so I decided to do a basic timeline activity. As we added the attack on the Twin Towers to our timeline, I explained to students that I remember exactly what I was doing when I found out. Not having been alive at the time, they were hanging on my every word. My Vice Principal walked in and I asked him to recount what he was doing at the time of the attack. He began to tell the students about living in Brooklyn for a few years and having friends who worked just down the street. The students were captivated and after he finished his story there were several hands raised in the air. These weren't the childish questions you might expect. These twelve-year-olds were asking about hatred, religion and violence. They were questions no one has the correct answer to but they promoted discussions that many of them had never considered. Our job is to make students think. How can we do this if we don't let them question?

Hermione asks a thoughtful question and any decent teacher would then take a moment to explain their objectives in more detail. Instead Professor Umbridge attempts to discredit Hermione, saying *"I'm afraid you're not qualified to decide what the 'whole point' of any class is...You will be learning about defensive spells in a secure, risk-free way—"⁵* Shouldn't students have a say in their education?

All Umbridge wants is complete control. To her dismay, her inadequate response only galvanizes the rest of the room into calling out their concerns in unison. She quickly becomes agitated that students won't raise their hands and shuts down their questions.

I do understand Umbridge's desire to micromanage. Many of us have her same expectation of hands being raised before they are called on to speak. I have micromanaging issues of my own. I make my students stack their chairs upside down on top of the table facing directly away from my desk. My students think I have OCD, but I explain to them that hair gets stuck to the bottom and it's disgusting staring at that while I work. Giving an honest explanation helps them understand why they are being forced to turn their chair to a specific direction. But Umbridge doesn't even try to explain her actions. She only asserts that this is what the Ministry wants, never considering what would be best for her students.

After failing to keep control of her class, Umbridge reiterates *"It is the view of the Ministry that a theoretical knowledge will be more than sufficient to get you through your examination, which, after all, is what school is all about."* [6] What school is all about? School is about bringing up lifelong learners who have the ability to think critically, communicate effectively, and become responsible citizens who make a positive contribution to their communities. School isn't about memorizing enough information to pass a test and look good on paper. Out of Umbridge's mouth this sounds crazy, yet schools unintentionally promote this. We force students to complete pointless worksheets, read uninteresting books, and take meaningless tests.

Teachers like Umbridge have driven the passion and imagination out of students. While teaching a peer mediation class, I decided to open each period with time for students to write in journals. One day I gave them a prompt that said, "Write a short story that begins with the phrase 'My hand trembled as I punched the number into the phone.'" I imagined their stories would be funny, scary and even inspirational. But they just stared at me. Some even asked if they were allowed to make it funny. Or asked what kind of phone it was. I was astounded. What happened to their creativity?

In their education, there has always been one right answer. They were so accustomed to teachers providing all the information that they were afraid to branch out. Children are naturally curious and enter school excited to learn. Somewhere along the way they had lost their sense of adventure and creativity. They ended up going through the motions, selecting C when told and not questioning or creating for themselves. The school system had failed them. Ken Robinson, author of Creative Schools and ingenious mind behind the number one watched TED talk on the same subject, writes, "If you run an education system based on standardization and conformity that suppress individuality, imagination, and creativity, don't be surprised if that's what it does." [7]

Professor Umbridge's lessons never get better than the first. For the rest of the school year she has them repeatedly sit down, put their wands away and read the next chapter in their textbook. Maybe she believes that if given the slightest freedom, students would turn their wands on her. Or maybe she thinks this is the only way to maintain quiet and order. Regardless of her beliefs, this is never going to help students after they graduate.

Harry points this out on the first day when he shouts *"And what good's theory going to be in the real world?"* Umbridge doesn't yell at him, but she does belittle him. *"This is school, Mr. Potter, not the real world…. Who do you imagine wants to attack children like yourselves?"*

Harry already has enough anger bubbling beneath the surface. He has practically been shouting at someone every few pages up to this point. It's almost as if Umbridge wants him to explode. Her sickly sweet voice sets him off and he shouts Lord Voldemort's name in response. Umbridge takes ten points from Harry but doesn't stop here. She continues to provoke him, stating in front of the whole class that Harry is a liar until he is made to shout again: *"It is NOT a lie!"*

She gives him detention but relentlessly continues on. And now Harry's had enough. Who can blame him? Everyone from his roommate to the Minister of Magic is calling him a liar and now his own teacher is antagonizing him in front of all his peers. He stands up this time and brings up Cedric's death: *"Voldemort killed him, and you know it."* [8] At last Professor Umbridge is done arguing, but it's too late. The damage is already done.

No good has ever come out of arguing with a student, and Umbridge is the reason Harry shouts. There are many better ways to deal with this disruption: Ask Harry to talk outside after class. Simply say the discussion is over and get back to the lesson. Or, here's a novel idea, actually teach the students the skills necessary to not only survive in the real world, but also pass her test.

Professor Umbridge sends Harry out of class with a note for his Head of House. In a move that betrays her later attempts at control, this shifts the authority away from Umbridge and over to Professor McGonagall. To Harry's surprise, McGonagall hands him a cookie and simply cautions him to behave better. This is exactly what Harry needed, but not what Umbridge wanted. In attempting what she thought was a demonstration of power, she only succeeds in demonstrating her insecurities. She can't handle simple questions from her students and her desire for complete control causes her to create impractical lessons that ultimately backfire. Her insulting objectives and silent reading lead to more disruptions than a fully interactive lesson ever would.

Umbridge's second Defense Against the Dark Arts lesson is just as thrilling as the first. As students daydream while pretending to read chapter two, Hermione's hand pops into the air again. This time Umbridge has devised a strategy for dealing with her inquisitiveness— walking over to her instead of staying seated. Hermione informs Umbridge she has already read the entire book and disagrees with the author's description of counterjinxes. With the rest of the class now completely ignoring their textbooks Umbridge quickly becomes annoyed and snaps back, *"Well, I'm afraid it is Mr. Sinkhard's opinion, and not yours, that matters within this classroom, Miss Granger."*[9]

Every student is unique and comes into our class with different experiences. It's important that students are able to evaluate sources, think critically and develop their own opinions especially in a world where false information is shared in an instant as if it were truth.

Umbridge is squandering Hermione's individuality. She wants students to memorize the theoretical approach to defensive spells and never apply it with their own skills and capabilities. A war is coming and her students don't know how to protect themselves. She is such a bad teacher that the students take it upon themselves to teach proper defensive skills in a Defensive Against the Dark Arts club of their own. Some skills are more important than rote memorization. The students in Umbridge's class know this and ours do too.

Umbridge's impractical lessons are driven from her insatiable desire for control, and she believes punishments are the greatest way to force students to submit, detention being her preferred method. Instead of using this time to mend the relationship, she doesn't talk to the student at all. There are some detentions where the only words exchanged between her and Harry are a stiff 'good evening' and 'good night.'

Be that as it may, the silence in Professor Umbridge's office is the best part of her detentions. She decides lines aren't malicious enough and develops a special quill that draws blood for ink and scratches words into the back of students' hands. Harry is required to repeat this over and over until the words "I must not tell lies" remain scarred as a permanent reminder of Umbridge's cruelty. To top it off, detentions with Umbridge are so long that Harry has no time to complete his homework assignments. He becomes more exhausted and falls further behind in his classes the more detentions he has to serve. This results in even more problems for him not only in Professor Umbridge's class, but others as well.

Teachers today don't have torturous magic quills, but our choices for punishment are sometimes astonishing. My first grade teacher tried to teach us the function of money and made us pay for basic items in the classroom with fake coins, including using the restroom. If you didn't have enough money saved up and still had to go, then you had to spend time in the "cage" (a square taped on the ground in the front of the room). I had a small bladder and a great fear to never be the center of attention. I don't remember much about my first grade teacher, but I do remember the shame of sitting in a puddle of warm pee because I was too frightened of the cage. When punishments leave scars—whether physical or mental—

we need to rethink our choices.

Even Umbridge's less sinister choices of punishment are idiotic. When Harry and George attack Malfoy for his rude comments about each of their parents, she bans the two of them and Fred (just for being George's twin) from Quidditch for life. There are legitimate reasons to keep students off of a sports team. This is not one of them. Quidditch is the only thing keeping Fred and George at school. Quidditch provides a release for the pent up anger that Harry has been building all school year. It keeps them all focused and sane. And Umbridge bans them. Fred and George retaliate by creating exponentially more mayhem the rest of the year. They choose to focus their energy not on their school work, as Umbridge would have preferred, but instead on their joke shop. Their timely exit out of Hogwarts is moved up and they never bother taking their tests and graduating at the end of the school year.

Professor Umbridge's desire for control isn't limited to her own classroom. She manages to convince the Minister of Magic that more government oversight is needed at Hogwarts and is gifted the title of High Inquisitor. This gives her the authority to evaluate other teachers and determine if their work is up to the Ministry's definition of quality. She interrupts lessons, degrades and nitpicks her way through Hogwarts classes, and oversteps boundaries left and right. Some teachers like McGonagall and Snape stand up to her and manage to continue teaching as they normally would. But others like Hagrid and Trelawney feel threatened. She uses her position of authority to bully and insult them, undermining their role as teachers in front of their students. Both are fired before term ends.

Her role of High Inquisitor also gives her the authority to pass nonsensical rules at Hogwarts. She bans sports teams and clubs. She doesn't allow students to read the Quibbler, instilling a desire in every student to find a copy of the outlawed magazine. And she forbids teachers from talking about anything outside their subject. This last Educational

Decree causes students like Lee Jordan to boldly point out that Umbridge has no right to tell Fred and George to stop playing Exploding Snap since it has nothing to do with her class.

Professor Umbridge just might have some control issues. I don't have a psychology degree but my friend is an A.P. Psychology teacher and she gives me Reese's when I fix her computer so I'm in her room often (I'm told this is operant conditioning) and I've picked up a few things. Issues like these don't manifest themselves from nowhere. Umbridge's parents divorced when she was a young girl and she felt her father, a janitor at the Ministry, wasn't ambitious enough. But there is no excuse great enough for how she treats people. A great teacher doesn't overpower their students—they empower them.

✴ MALICIOUS ✴

Prior to Professor Umbridge's arrival to Hogwarts, a student named Cedric Diggory was murdered by Lord Voldemort. The students are immediately released back home for the summer without the chance to hear the real story. They don't have the opportunity to mourn together and begin to heal. On the first day of classes the subject surrounding his death inevitably comes up again. Umbridge refuses to believe Harry about Voldemort and begins to argue with him in class:

> "So, according to you, Cedric Diggory dropped dead of his own accord, did he?" Harry asked, his voice shaking.
>
> ...
>
> "Cedric Diggory's death was a tragic accident," she said coldly.
> "It was murder," said Harry. [10]

Professor Umbridge has the opportunity to help her students grieve and help them understand a complex situation. All she needed to be was thoughtful, kind and compassionate—all things she is not. Instead, she sends Harry out of class.

I'm curious what was said after Harry left. Did she continue to tell the class more lies? Did she ignore the situation and make them get back to work immediately? Did she make an example of Harry? All of these responses are wrong. I know it has been months since Cedric's death, but I can still picture my students' faces in the weeks after one of my students was killed. His absence in the classroom could be felt. A heavy silence when his chosen topic for a project was skipped over during presentations. The look on a student's face when she was passing back work and had to walk one of his papers back to me because I forgot to take it out of the graded work pile. Just like them, Harry is obviously still hurting. He needs help and Umbridge gives him detention.

One year I arrived to school on a Friday with the intention of having a perfectly normal day. I walked out to talk with some of my coworkers and one of them asked me if I had a specific student in my class. I replied a bit quizzically, "Yeah, why?"

"He was murdered last night." Those words bounced around my brain for a few minutes. Murdered. That is a word for mystery novels and crime shows. Murder has no place in my life. I struggled to stay in the moment. I managed to reply, "He's in my class. He brought me chocolate." I felt I had to justify the reason I was freaking out.

When I got back to my classroom, I pulled up the news article on my computer. The headline was so specific and yet didn't help to make it any more real: "17 Year-Old Killed in Shooting." Only small details stuck out to me even though I read through the short article more than 5 times: Shot 2 to 3 times. In front of a church. He was a student.

At this point I was crying uncontrollably. My friend walked in and asked if I was okay. Speaking was difficult without making some kind of whimpering animal sound, so I nodded my head. Out of fear she would begin crying herself, she barely looked at me and said, "You better hurry up and get your shit together." When we were texting later, I made fun of the way she consoles people (she told me to get my shit together not once, but twice); she sent me this:

> Two reasons I told you to get your shit together... 1. So I didn't cry with you or for you (selfish) 2. Your students needed you (selfless). I just figured you didn't want to be a blubbery mess... emotional—yes, real—yes, a hot mess—no. So you're welcome.

From an outsider's perspective, this may seem harsh, but this was her way of telling me she cared and her attempt to make me laugh. Others had given me hugs or tried to encourage me, but this only made it worse. Tori's words were exactly what I needed to survive. The whole rest of the day I kept repeating her advice to myself. 'Get your shit together. You can do this. Tori's right, you need to get your shit together.'

Fourth period was my loudest class that year and not a single one of them was talking as they entered. They sat in their assigned seats—as if that even mattered—half of them crying, half of them staring straight forward not really seeing. One student walked straight into my arms and I held her for a full minute as she sobbed into my sweatshirt. All I could say was "I know. I know. I know." I couldn't keep my tears at bay and I didn't try to. These students knew I loved him. It would be impersonal to act like it didn't affect me as much as it affected them. Like Tori said, I didn't want to be a blubbery mess, but emotional was appropriate.

The bell rang and I walked up to the front of the class still silently crying. What was I supposed to do with thirty grieving teenagers for fifty-five minutes? I sat on top of the table in the front of the room, grabbed a tissue and started talking.

"I don't know what to say. I'm the adult. Your teacher. I want to fix this situation. I want to have the answers for you—that's my job. But I don't even know how to react to this myself. All I know is that this... sucks."

I paused as I gathered myself. The class was silent still except for the occasional sob. "I loved Andrew." A student in the back dropped his head at this point and began crying. He didn't know Andrew was the person who would never walk through that door again. He hadn't seen it on social media. He hadn't heard it whispered in first period. He didn't know. And I was the one who had to break the news to him.

"I loved Andrew. You all know that. He brought me a Reese's yesterday. He knew I loved it and dropped it on my desk like it was nothing. I can still hear his chuckle and picture that giant wad of keys dangling around his neck."

I was rambling. I don't ramble. I didn't know what else to do except to share in their grief.

"I can hear him say 'Ms. Deeee' and laugh. Like everything was a joke."

Andrew was killed on March 31. I felt like it was some elaborate April fools joke. That he was going to walk through that door again with some more Reese's and I would hear his unique laugh and it would all be okay. It wasn't.

We spent the rest of the period crying and sharing stories. There was even some laughter. We remembered how he always wanted to touch girls' hair. How he would walk in late with a burger and the whole class would smell it and be jealous. One student told us how he convinced her that it was important to take the SAT just the day before. I gave more hugs that day than I had all year.

It took us many days to fully recover and get back into a normal routine. I moved their seats the following week but intentionally left Andrew's seat open without drawing attention to it. Students used chalk to write RIP Drew all over the school. These things helped.

We moved on, but I couldn't help but pull out that melted Reese's he had given me the day he died. He had come into class and said "Ms. Deee, I got you chocolate but it melted in my car." He laughed in that distinct laugh I can still hear but can't imitate. I pulled it out less and less as the year went on.

Andrew will always have an impact on me and the way I teach. We never know what will happen to our students when they walk out the door. I can't remember the last thing I told him that day. I hope it was something positive. I hope I was encouraging and that he knew how much I loved having him in my class. I hope I thanked him for the Reese's on that last day. I'll never know.

You never know what type of day you will have before walking into school. I pray I never have another day like that. I couldn't handle it magically. I barely handled it. There were moments that next week and the week after when I couldn't focus. I wasn't being an effective teacher. I tried to be present and understanding for my students but some days it wasn't happening.

While I didn't handle it perfectly, I was at least understanding of my students' needs. I gave more time for students to complete their assignments if they asked for it. I let them step outside whenever they needed. I let them spend more time in class sharing stories and talking if it felt like we all needed a break for the day. This lasted for weeks. Andrew was not forgotten, but as a class we moved back to our normal routine again. I felt closer to this class than some of my others that year. We had been through a tragedy that pushed us together.

Professor Dumbledore's response to Cedric's death is infinitely more considerate than Umbridge's and is what I wish us all to emulate. At the end of *Goblet of Fire*, after Harry has physically recovered from his trip to the graveyard and the school has gathered in the Great Hall for their last feast. The room was missing its usual decorations and instead black drapes lined the walls in a sign of respect for Cedric. As Dumbledore gets up to speak to a subdued crowd, he turns to address the Hufflepuffs in particular, as they feel the loss the greatest:

> *"There is much that I would like to say to you all tonight,"*
> *said Dumbledore, "but I must first acknowledge the loss of a*
> *very fine person, who should be sitting here," he gestured*

toward the Hufflepuffs, "enjoying our feast with us. I would like you all, please, to stand, and raise your glasses, to Cedric Diggory."

Professor Dumbledore continues his speech after everyone is seated with more kind words for Cedric. He explains how Cedric embodies all the character traits of Helga Hufflepuff, the most generous of the founders. Then he does something that is shocking to the student body and completely against the Ministry of Magic's wishes—he tells them the truth.

> *"It is possible that some of your parents will be horrified that I have done so — either because they will not believe that Lord Voldemort has returned, or because they think I should not tell you so, young as you are. It is my belief, however, that the truth is generally preferable to lies, and that any attempt to pretend that Cedric died as the result of an accident, or some sort of blunder of his own, is an insult to his memory."[11]*

After Andrew's death my students were weary that I wasn't telling them everything I knew. In truth, my students often knew more than me since they were on social media and in contact with Andrew's immediate family. The school wasn't excellent at passing down information.

I admire Professor Dumbledore's response to tell his students the truth. He opens himself to immediate backlash—his name (and Harry's by association) is dragged through the mud by the Daily Prophet. But through it all he stands by what he thinks is right and tells the students the truth of Lord Voldemort's return and Cedric's murder.

I'm not recommending outright defying a district mandate, but I do believe that students can handle more than we give them credit for. I certainly witnessed this firsthand with my students. They helped guide me through Andrew's death more than I had anticipated. They were kind and considerate as they sat by me at Andrew's funeral, as we met as a class to honor him at the candle-lighting vigil at the spot of his passing and as we returned to normal routines in the classroom.

In this moment, Umbridge fails her students. We can't always say the right things in times like these, but there will always be things we should never say. Umbridge has an entire summer to plan an appropriate response. When the moment arises, she is inconsiderate and rude. Worst of all, she lies to her students and acts as if Cedric's death should be brushed away and forgotten. There are many things I would do over if given the chance. You never wake up thinking you will go to work and hear your student has been murdered. I wish I had remembered Dumbledore's words at the end of *Goblet of Fire* so I could have used them that day:

> *"Remember Cedric. Remember, if the time should come when you have to make a choice between what is right and what is easy, remember what happened to a boy who was good, and kind, and brave, because he strayed across the path of Lord Voldemort. Remember Cedric Diggory."* [12]

So to my 4th period class: Remember Andrew.

✳ ✳ ✳

Sadly, the mishandling of Cedric's death is far from the only derisive thing that Umbridge does all year. She discriminates against Hagrid and Firenze because they are "half-breeds." She creates the Inquisitorial Squad and enables hand-picked students to inflict further abuse on their peers. And amidst paranoid fears of insubordination, she tries to slip Harry Veritaserum and even attempts to use the illegal Cruciatus Curse on him. Her first instinct is always self-preservation and self-empowerment. If a student gets in her way then she will use him as a shield, literally. The students hate her more than anyone.

All of these things are awful. We can agree, she is terrible. But in most cases teachers are not going to abuse their students physically, use them as human shields, or try to drug them. These things are all absurd. What we need to be concerned about are the small things that often go unnoticed.

Professor Umbridge sits in on the guidance meetings that the Heads of Houses have with their students and outright dismisses their career goals. During Harry's meeting with McGonagall she bluntly tells him that he will never accomplish his dream of becoming an Auror. Harry is the hero of the stories, but he still doubts his own abilities. Now, his dream of becoming an Auror is being shot down by his own teacher and someone who works for the Ministry.

After I began taking the classes necessary to become a teacher, someone close to me, who was a teacher himself, told me I haven't shown the aptitude for working with kids. His proof was the limited interactions I had had with his own young children. Even though I wanted to teach older students, this still stung. I had pursued my dream of being a teacher for as long as I could remember and now I was being told by a teacher that I wouldn't be successful. Fortunately, I had family to encourage me and an intense desire to prove people wrong. Instead of hindering my pursuit, after a bit of recovery, this emotional setback only fueled my determination. Harry, perhaps with the same desire to prove Umbridge wrong, does become an Auror and even advances to head of the department. Without support, however, these conversations could have been detrimental to both our dreams. We need to remember that many of our students don't have these support systems at home and our words can carry immense weight.

As I think back on my own school experiences, trying to recall the Umbridge-like teachers, I remember having a teacher in elementary school who would throw desks out the door and make his sixth grade students walk outside, pick them up and sit there the rest of the day no matter the weather. If you were lucky enough to keep your desk inside then you could still be forced to sit at the 'dunces table.' I remember spending hours at home scouring an old cookie tin full of half-used, broken crayons looking for the perfect shade of brown out of fear that the picture I was coloring of a Great Horned Owl would be incorrect and would place me next in line for banishment. I learned nothing from that class but the limits of my stress when working under conditions of fear. This teacher retired eventually after many years of distinguished service. He was considered by many to be one of the greats. In a system where we value control over creativity, these are the types of teachers that will be rewarded.

The real frightening Umbridge's of the world aren't teaching (I hope). But there will always be some teachers with Umbridge-like characteristics that may squeak by. In fact, there are moments when my inner Umbridge skulks about my own classroom uninvited. I snap at students when I'm having a bad day. I dismiss questions that don't pertain to our topic even when they are thoughtful, important ones. And I argue with students when I should listen. This is the real concern. Professor Umbridge is a vindictive, power-hungry, prejudiced woman, but she shows us that we need to be wary of our own teaching styles even if we never approach her level of malevolence.

Defense Against the Dark Arts is supposed to prepare students to protect themselves against ruthless magical attacks and is paramount to their survival of the upcoming war. Over the last five years, the misfortunate students at Hogwarts receive mundane, arrogant and malicious teachers. Only Professor Lupin completely exists outside of these categories. But it is Professor Umbridge who proves to be the worst of them all. Where Quirrell and Lockhart only hinder student learning, Professor Umbridge sets them back entirely. In order to have any semblance of success, students have to take learning into their own hands. Harry's growth and impact as leader of Dumbledore's Army is truly the only positive to come out of Umbridge's despicable reign at Hogwarts.

PART V: HARRY AND THE HEADMASTER

HARRY POTTER

*

PROFESSOR DUMBLEDORE

HARRY POTTER

Practical   *   Empowering

*"That was quite good," Harry lied, but when she raised her
eyebrows he said, "Well, no, it was lousy, but I know you can do it
properly, I was watching from over there..."*[1]

THE D.A.

Harry Potter isn't a prefect or a top student at Hogwarts. He's prone to flashes of anger and doesn't even finish all seven years. Harry is not a teacher and he never becomes one. Other than being famous for surviving Lord Voldemort's attacks, Harry is, by all measures, an average student. But in *Order of the Phoenix* he gets the opportunity to do something great beyond his unwanted fame. During Professor Umbridge's horrid time at Hogwarts, Harry and his peers form a club called Dumbledore's Army (the D.A.) so they can properly learn how to defend themselves against the Dark Arts. Thanks to a passionate speech, they choose Harry, a mediocre fifth-year student, as their leader.

Much has been written about Harry's character and heroic actions. He is extremely patient with eccentric characters like Dobby, befriends outcasts like Luna Lovegood and trusts Hagrid even though he's several times his height and only just broke down a door to introduce himself at midnight. We all know Harry is courageous and virtuous. But... would he make a good professor?

Rather than analyze every opportunity Harry has to impart wisdom, this chapter will only focus on his role as an instructor while leading Dumbledore's Army. For six months Harry leads his classmates through a variety of hands-on, practical approaches to Defense Against the Dark Arts during which members of the D.A. learn more than in most of their previous classes.

✳ PRACTICAL ✳

In defiance of Professor Umbridge's theoretical approach to teaching Defense Against the Dark Arts, Harry, Ron and Hermione form Dumbledore's Army to help students learn defensive skills. Hermione feels Harry has shown the most results and aptitude in defending himself over the years, making him the perfect candidate to lead. She explains, *"We need a teacher, a proper one, who can show us how to use the spells and correct us if we've gone wrong."*[2] With the exception of the deviously charming Lockhart, who fooled even Mrs. Weasley, Hermione is critical of all teachers. She even quits Divination in the middle of the year. So for her to suggest Harry could be not only a teacher, but a 'proper' one is some of the highest praise she has given.

Harry denies having any more skill than Ron. And Hermione beats him in almost every subject. Since we, as readers, are privileged to his inner thoughts, we see firsthand that he's nowhere near the best student Hogwarts has to offer. He often has side conversations and daydreams during teachers' instructions, falls asleep in class and copies most of his homework. Honestly, without Hermione, he wouldn't have survived. Harry can't believe anyone would want him to teach. After some consideration, however, he decides he is at least willing to share his knowledge.

I appreciate his humility. One of the reasons I love Harry as a hero is his belief that he isn't the savior. He knows he has only been successful because of help (and a bit of cheating) along the way. Whether saving the wizarding world or teaching a classroom full of students, help is always needed.

In my first year of teaching, I isolated myself. I never asked for help and I never received it. I spent more days that first year stressed and overwhelmed than needed. No one shared their curriculum with me or checked to make sure I wasn't staying in my classroom until it was dark every night. I needed help and no one was there to rescue me, but I only have myself to blame. I never ventured out of my dungeon or sought other teachers' opinions. I was too intimidated, but I didn't have to be. Teaching became something greater once I opened my classroom to others and began to collaborate.

As Harry plans lessons for the D.A., he receives help not only from Ron and Hermione, but Sirius and Lupin as well. After some guidance, he decides to focus on the specific skills necessary for self-protection. In contrast to Professor Umbridge's class, Harry decides the D.A. will concentrate on the practical application. Essentially, his teaching philosophy is take everything she does and do the exact opposite. He starts with a basic spell, Expelliarmus, and works their way up towards casting more difficult spells like a Patronus, giving his peers plenty of time and space to practice each one.

Zacharias Smith, feeling that reviewing fundamental skills is beneath him, protests that the Disarming Charm is not going to help them against You-Know-Who. We have all had a Zacharias Smith in our class. Sometimes we have multiple. They're the students that are never pleased, yet perfectly happy to stop the flow of any lesson. They roll their eyes, fold their arms and throw mini teenage tantrums. My latest Zacharias Smith likes to proclaim loud enough for the whole class to hear, "Since I already know this and can complete this assignment in five minutes, I'm going to the bathroom."

Harry is no stranger to sarcasm. There's a part of me that wants him to say the things that boil up inside every time a student obnoxiously objects to my lessons. Perhaps a classic 'Oh! Good for you!' or maybe a subtle golf clap or an overdramatic demonstration of the door. But Harry does what any good teacher would do, he responds to the outburst with calm assurance. He informs Smith that Expelliarmus saved his own life against Lord Voldemort last June. Everyone is quiet while Smith sits there opening his mouth, but no noise comes out. Harry has won this disagreement by providing clear facts. Despite that, he can't help but throw in, *"But if you think it's beneath you, you can leave."*[3] There's the cheeky Harry we know and love!

As they begin to practice, it quickly becomes apparent that starting with the basics is all but necessary. Even in the Room of Requirement's cozy and safe environment, many of the students fail to disarm their opponents. Harry doesn't waste any time forcing his classmates to read. Instead with each lesson, he informs the D.A. members of the spell they will practice, pairs them off to begin, then walks about the room correcting any mistakes. This is the practice they need to help prepare them for what's out there: Lord Voldemort and his Death Eaters.

Sometimes we focus too much on what students need to know inside of school. Covering the standards, passing the tests and achieving high grades are great, but they will never experience these after graduation. Lord Voldemort isn't waiting outside your school's gates ready to snatch unsuspecting students. But the real world is. Some want to go to college but don't know how they will afford tuition. Many don't know how to pay taxes, how rent works, about credit, or even where to register to vote. These are all very practical skills that our students need to learn and many no longer get this instruction at home.

Nontraditional skills like these often get overlooked, but there are more typical academic skills that are frequently forgotten or pushed aside. I find that many students enter my classroom not knowing how to write. One year I had a group of junior high students who had never heard of a topic sentence and couldn't write a full paragraph. Just as Harry does with the D.A. members, I had to start with the basics. I decided to experiment with a variety of strategies to help my students grow as writers. The first is called Writing to Think and it was a great way to take the pressure off of formal writing.[4] Students write for an allotted amount of time and jot down whatever pops into their head. I let my students write in any direction on the paper and never graded for grammar or content—only participation.

I used this strategy as an introduction lesson to a formal written response on American colonist's tactics during the Revolutionary War. I gave them a few fun prompts to begin, starting with: Someone is on a diet and decides to eat junk food one day out of the week. Is it cheating? A player intentionally takes a dive in a soccer game to draw the foul. Is it cheating? Then I moved them closer to events that took place during the Revolutionary War. Is it cheating to attack an enemy at night while they sleep? Is using spies cheating? Is using guerrilla warfare tactics cheating? And finally, is targeting the officers of the opposing army cheating?

I forced students to respond to each question for one full minute then had them share their opinions out loud. After putting their thoughts down on paper, their verbal responses were more developed. At the end of the lesson I gave them their official prompt: Did the American colonists cheat in the Revolutionary War? For the first time they were able to write thoughtful responses backed with evidence.

Another strategy I used that year was something we called pen-pal notebooks. I wanted to make writing more interactive and purposeful so I bought spiral bound notebooks and wrote the numbers 1-30 on the front. Each student from my three seventh-grade classes was assigned a number.

They would read notes from their pen-pals and respond every day.

We started each day with an opinion question that related to our topic like 'If you had to choose, which Chinese Dynasty would you want to live in and why?' The student in the first class was responsible for writing the question at the top and then responding. The second class would respond to the first students, agreeing or disagreeing and explaining. Then the third student responded to both students before them. It took some training. I was concerned that weak writers would be ashamed, but assigning each student a number kept the activity anonymous. Over time, everyone—no matter their ability—progressed. The stronger writers continued to improve while also setting an example for the weaker ones.

The idea that students had a response waiting for them when they got to class made writing more exciting. And the public nature of the assignment made them double check their work and put more thought into their writing. This helped prepare my students for actual conversations they may have in the future in an online format. Whether through email or social media, these students are going to experience forum posts at some point. Teaching them how to appropriately respond to their classmates and politely disagree was a great lesson for them to learn. While they may not remember the Chinese dynasties they wrote about to their pen-pals that day, I'm sure these writing skills will endure.

Even though some students feel the spells are beneath them, Harry chooses the skills he feels will be most important for the D.A.'s survival in the fight against Lord Voldemort. Even Ernie McMillan, who highly values his grades and social status at Hogwarts, says, *"this is really important, possibly more important than anything else we'll do this year, even with our O.W.L.s coming up!"*[5] What practical skills are important enough to make your students shout like Ernie?

✳ EMPOWERING ✳

Lessons with the D.A. only work because of Harry's disposition and temperament. His positivity helps to get all types of students from multiple Hogwarts houses to come together and be successful. From annoying students like Zacharias Smith to top students like Hermione Granger, all members of the D.A. make great progress. If Draco Malfoy had been their leader, his negativity would hinder their growth. Even Hermione wouldn't have been as successful. D.A. meetings with her in charge would most likely end with Neville in tears. Harry has his flaws, but his positivity shines through in all interactions with the D.A. Whenever he can, he walks alongside the students and encourages them until they master any given spell.

In their first meeting, Neville Longbottom is left without a partner so Harry practices with him. As Harry's eyes wander to monitor other students' progress, Neville manages to disarm him. He's ecstatic as this is the first time he has ever managed to disarm an opponent. Harry chooses not to mention to Neville that most attackers will be paying attention to the duel, but instead congratulates him. This is an important moment in Harry's short-lived teaching career. He can choose to either be brutally honest with Neville (something Ron or Hermione would have done) or encourage him. Sometimes a positive mentality can be the best thing to push our students forward.

After assessing students' ability to cast Expelliarmus, he stops the class to address his concerns. He tells them *"That wasn't bad, but there's definitely room for improvement"*[6] which is teacher-speak for 'that was awful.' While he doesn't demonstrate proper wand movement for the entire class, he does walk around the room providing individual feedback as they continue practicing. His first lesson runs smoothly, and students learn an important skill as time flies by. His only noticeable flaw is lack of time management, needing Hermione to remind him when to dismiss everyone.

As his classmates progress throughout the year, the D.A. helps Harry stay focused and survive Umbridge's awfully boring lessons. With the books written from Harry's perspective, we never get insight into other teachers' motivation. But with Harry we get a rare glimpse into a 'teacher's' mind. As he sits in Umbridge's class pretending to read, he remembers:

> "How Neville had successfully disarmed Hermione, how Colin Creevey had mastered the Impediment Jinx after three meetings' hard effort, how Parvati Patil had produced such a good Reductor Curse that she had reduced the table carrying all the Sneakoscopes to dust."[7]

It's obvious that his students' success brings him more joy than anything else that year.

In my worst times, Harry's internal thoughts remind me that teaching should bring out these emotions. If I'm not leaving work with these feelings, then it's time to make a change. In my sixth year, I hit a sort of slump. I was becoming complacent with my lessons and found myself longing for summer. The days dragged by. My students had been asking for weeks for the chance to debate, but I wasn't feeling up to planning something so involved. Finally I gave in and planned a debate with the overarching question 'Are violent protests ever justified?' As students each took turns passionately providing evidence, including one girl who ended her rebuttal with "We need to remember that to be human is to be humane," I was reminded, once again, why I love teaching.

Before the holidays, Harry, unlike me, still has the energy needed to plan interactive lessons. He has students practice all the spells they had already covered, knowing it would be pointless starting something new before the break. Harry swells with pride again as he sees his classmates perform perfect spells that he had taught them. By this point Neville is rapidly improving under Harry's instruction. As they move on to Shield Charms, only Hermione manages to learn the new skill quicker than him. Neville's rapid growth proves Harry's practical teaching philosophy is superior to Umbridge's theoretical one. Neville has new motivation with the release of Bellatrix Lestrange (his parent's tormentor), but Harry deserves credit for channeling Neville's determination into action.

The Patronus Charm (an advanced spell that dispels dementors) is the last spell the D.A. covers before Umbridge discovers their meetings. With Harry's guidance, many students are able to produce corporeal Patronuses. This is a skill that Professor Lupin thought would be too difficult for even himself to teach. And yet Harry manages to teach much of the D.A. this advanced piece of magic. As their spirit-like animals bound around the classroom, Harry reminds them that the Patronus Charm is much easier in a brightly lit classroom than when facing the dreary abyss of a dementor's kiss, but this doesn't stop him from being proud.

As their meetings come to an end and Umbridge's Inquisitorial Squad rounds up the members of the D.A., Harry's only concern is for his peers. He's worried about what Mrs. Weasley will say to Ron, if Hermione will be expelled and that Neville wouldn't be able to continue progressing in Defense Against the Dark Arts. To put others' needs above one's own is the mark of a truly caring leader.

* * *

For Harry's inexperience, he has extraordinary teaching abilities. As a leader he responds positively to Zacharias Smith's accusations and stops the twins from disrupting lessons. Even though he is their peer (and younger than several members), he earns their respect. He plans effective differentiated lessons, manages a class full of students of various ages and houses all while being consistently calm and supportive. During meetings, Harry walks around the classroom more than most Hogwarts teachers to monitor his classmates' progress. And to top it off, he even completes basic formative assessments that help him determine the best way to guide students to mastery of each specific spell.

If Harry had not pursued a career with the Ministry of Magic, he would have made an excellent teacher. In Professor Umbridge's opening speech she talks about being called to the noble profession of teaching. But it is clear that Harry is the one who is called to teach. During his last D.A.

meeting he thinks to himself:

> *"He sometimes felt that he was living for the hours he spent in the Room of the Requirement, working hard but thoroughly enjoying himself at the same time, swelling with pride as he looked around at his fellow D.A. members and saw how far they had come."*[8]

In six months Harry does what most other Defense Against the Dark Arts teachers failed to do before him—teach students to defend themselves.

PROFESSOR DUMBLEDORE

WISE * RECEPTIVE * TRUSTING

"Help will always be given at Hogwarts to those who ask for it." [1]

Professor Dumbledore is one of the most complex and fascinating characters from the Harry Potter series. As his chocolate frog card states, he is famous for his defeat of Gellert Grindelwald, his work on alchemy and his discovery of the twelve uses of dragon's blood. How could there possibly be twelve different uses for blood? I wonder if he had to update the list to thirteen after Slughorn uses dragon's blood as a way to fake his death. Because of his prodigious skills, Dumbledore is often consulted by the government for advice and even turns down the job of Minister of Magic, knowing he isn't suited to hold power.

For the duration of Harry's education, he is only seen as headmaster at Hogwarts, but he was once a renowned professor, and continued to be a mentor and teacher to many students long after he took on this responsibility. His long beard, half-moon spectacles and piercing blue eyes give off the appearance that he is performing Occlumency on anyone his gaze holds. But it isn't his personal accolades or physical attributes that make him great. It is his willingness to trust his staff, care for his students, and admit his mistakes that make him successful. Professor Dumbledore is one of the greatest examples of a literary teacher, and yet he is the professor we spend the least amount of time with in a traditional classroom.

✳ WISE ✳

Professor Dumbledore's mind and skills are as legendary as he is. As a student at Hogwarts he earned every prize offered and immediately after graduating was in correspondence with some of the brightest witches and wizards of his time. But his intelligence isn't an in-your-face, know-it-all display. Sure, he has moments where he points out his brilliance, but he does this in such a humble manner that everyone (other than Cornelius Fudge) feels bolstered by his presence rather than inferior in comparison. Harry's first glimpse of Dumbledore is when he stands up to give a speech just before the students are about to eat in *Sorcerer's Stone*. Dumbledore welcomes them to Hogwarts and says *"Before we begin our banquet, I would like to say a few words. And here they are: Nitwit! Blubber! Oddment! Tweak!"* That's it. After the long Sorting, that's all he says before he sits back down and allows them to eat. Harry, as a new student and new to this whole wizard stuff, looks puzzled and turns to Percy to ask if he is mad. Percy replies, *"He's a genius! Best wizard in the world! But he is a bit mad, yes."*[2]

Imagine being a new student at Hogwarts like Harry and the rest of the first years. You just left your family for the semester at the age of eleven, walked through a wall, traveled on a train, met new people, took a boat to a castle—a *magical* castle. I know I would be starving and certainly not ready to listen to a long boring speech from the headmaster. Dumbledore's use of humor in this moment isn't mad, it is the perfect touch of authority and wisdom. He follows this same example in other years simply saying "*tuck in,*" allowing the students to fill their bellies before they have to listen to rules and guidelines. This helps win the students over. They now associate Dumbledore with a smile and good food. When he speaks again, they'll be listening even more attentively than before.

Thankfully, Dumbledore's knowledge of his students' needs extends beyond just food. At the end of *Sorcerer's Stone,* Dumbledore awards Ron, Hermione, Harry and Neville extra house points adding up to a total greater than Slytherin's to win the House Cup. The order of the points is extremely important. Although Neville earned the fewest points of these four young Gryffindors, his points were awarded last. Dumbledore does this quite intentionally. He knows the difficulty of standing up to one's friends as it took him several years to face his own, Grindelwald. By this point, Neville has been picked on by both students and teachers. He lost his toad, failed several assignments, lost his toad again and even broke his wrist. By the end of the year, he has not won a single point for Gryffindor. By giving Neville these points last, Dumbledore makes him the hero, the person who won Gryffindor the House Cup. Sure, he's not winning any favors with the Slytherins, but Neville needs the assurances more.

Dumbledore's greatest teaching moments, however, come when he works with Harry individually. He seems to save his most thoughtful discussions for the end of each school year. While they are short in comparison to the amount of time Harry spends with his other professors, they are perhaps more important to Harry's development than all his other lessons combined.

At the end of Harry's first year he comes face to face with Voldemort, successfully protects the Sorcerer's Stone and begins asking deep questions about life and death. He's concerned that Nicolas Flamel will die now that the Stone is destroyed, but Dumbledore tells him, "*to the well-organized mind, death is but the next great adventure.*"[3] I'm surprised more isn't said about the fact that Harry just killed one of his teachers. Sure, Quirrell was attempting to murder him, but we don't get to see the affect this death has on Harry. He literally killed someone with his bare hands! Perhaps it is for the best that he doesn't dwell on it. Harry doesn't immediately understand Dumbledore's insightful quote on the afterlife. When he recites this later for Ron and Hermione, Ron dismisses the assertion, saying Dumbledore is crazy. But death is a constant in Harry's life. From his first memory, he had to deal with the loss of his parents, and as the years pass death comes to greet his friends more and more. Harry needs someone in his life who is willing to have these discussions with him and who better than Professor Dumbledore.

The subject of death comes up again at the end of *Prisoner of Azkaban*. After plotting revenge all year, Harry ends up saving Peter Pettigrew's life instead of killing him. Harry is concerned that his actions will directly lead to Voldemort's return to power. But Dumbledore assures him that saving a person's life, especially someone who has wronged you, is a noble trait. This reunion with his dad's old friends, however, makes Harry feel a renewed loss for his parents. Dumbledore tells Harry that the dead never truly leave us, pointing out that Harry and his father share the same Patronus. He helps Harry realize that his dad would have also saved Pettigrew and that the people we care about most are always within ourselves.

Death becomes more prominent in Harry's life when he witnesses a friend's murder. Against the Ministry's wishes, in Harry's fourth year, Dumbledore tells the students the truth about Cedric Diggory's passing and calls for unity in the upcoming war. Unlike Professor Umbridge's malicious approach to a student's grief, Dumbledore addresses Harry's pain, sounding more like Yoda when he explains that *"Understanding is the first step to acceptance, and only with acceptance can there be recovery."*[4] It takes Harry more time to heal from this experience than others. Who can blame him? He had to watch Cedric die in front of him! His lingering nightmares indicate that he probably needs more counseling than he is given. Are there therapists in the wizarding world? Even without Muggle therapy, Dumbledore's words make him determined to fight for what is right even though he knows the path forward won't be easy.

But in Harry's fifth year, his sorrow only continues to grow. Dumbledore consoles Harry over the death of Sirius, telling him the fact that he can feel pain is his greatest strength. After the death of so many close to him, his godfather's loss is felt the most. For the first time, Harry becomes genuinely angry at Dumbledore. He shouts and tears apart his office, but Dumbledore remains calm when he admits that he made a huge mistake. He feels the flaw in his plan was caring too much for Harry and that's why he distanced himself and hid the truth about his parents' death. However, as Dumbledore has been teaching Harry for the last five years, the ability to love isn't a weakness. In both the fight against Voldemort and their endeavors at Hogwarts, it is their greatest strength.

We may not always get the opportunity to discuss personal matters with our students such as the loss of life, but we can intentionally plan thoughtful discussions into any lesson. Dumbledore shows us that these deep conversations are the ones that can most impact a student's life. In *Chamber of Secrets*, Harry is struggling through an identity crisis. He is concerned that he shares many of the same characteristics and belongs in the same house as Lord Voldemort. Dumbledore tells him that he does exhibit the Slytherin qualities of resourcefulness and determination, but *"It is our choices... that show what we truly are, far more than our abilities."*[5] This is a key moment for Harry. He will go on to be ostracized by the wizarding community, frowned upon for refusing to kill and just like any teenager, misunderstood. Coming from the world's most talented wizard, hearing that choice matters more than power is encouraging.

Our students don't have magic wands and weren't born with lightning bolt scars, but they are struggling with the same issues as Harry. Many of them are trying to overcome grief and all of them are developing their individuality. Like Dumbledore, we need to be willing to address these deep topics.

I have always credited this series with playing a huge role in shaping my life and work. But I realized that most of this advice comes straight from Professor Dumbledore. He's the one who Harry turns to at the end of each year and his death is the reason Harry seems so lost for most of book seven. Dumbledore teaches Harry and us alongside him about true bravery, the power of love, and the importance of believing in ourselves. While we don't get to see him teach any specific spells, his discussions do more to shape Harry into a compassionate hero than any other professor.

✳ RECEPTIVE ✳

Professor Dumbledore shows us that we can't call ourselves wise if we aren't humble about our knowledge. Despite spending more time with his other professors, Harry feels Dumbledore is less likely to mock one of his theories than someone like Professor McGonagall. In *Prisoner of Azkaban*, Harry is comfortable enough to admit to Dumbledore that he thought he saw his dad produce the Patronus Charm that saved his life, knowing that Dumbledore would never laugh at him. The reason Harry trusts Dumbledore's wisdom is because he welcomes everyone's ideas and admits his mistakes. He even points this out in *Chamber of Secrets* when he threatens repercussions upon Harry and Ron if they break one more rule, only to realize how necessary their rule-breaking was to save Ginny, telling them, *"the best of us must sometimes eat our words."*

Professor Dumbledore realizes that a student's curiosity is what helps them truly learn. The only time he seems to answer a question untruthfully is in *Sorcerer's Stone* when he is asked what he sees in the Mirror of Erised. Dumbledore responds with *"I see myself holding a pair of thick, woolen socks... One can never have enough socks."* A clear lie, even though Dumbledore tells Harry at the end of the year, *"I shall answer your questions unless I have a very good reason not to, in which case I beg you'll forgive, I shall not, of course, lie."*[6] Perhaps it's a partial truth, because who wouldn't want more socks?

PROFESSOR DUMBLEDORE

However, even as a blatant lie, this is a clever response. No teacher should be required to share such personal information with a student, even if that student does go on to save the world. In my early years of teaching I would tell my students I was 98 years old every time they asked my age. This added Dumbledore-esque humor to my class without revealing my inexperience. If Dumbledore or I would have berated our students for asking questions we didn't want to answer, then they would feel less comfortable approaching us with real issues in the future.

The closest we get to seeing Professor Dumbledore in a traditional classroom is in *Half-Blood Prince* during his individual lessons with Harry. Dumbledore remains set on helping Harry develop his own knowledge rather than simply imparting Harry with existing information. When Harry enters Dumbledore's office on their first night of these meetings, he is curious about what Dumbledore will teach. Maybe he believes they'll be similar to his lessons with the D.A.. He is a little disappointed, however, when no space is cleared for dueling practice. But Dumbledore doesn't teach Harry wand movement or advanced spells. No, he believes the most important weapon in defeating the Dark Lord is knowledge of Voldemort's past. As a history teacher, I highly approve. I would argue, however, that Dumbledore teaches him far more than just information about You-Know-Who—he also teaches him how to think for himself.

This is a key characteristic of Dumbledore's teaching style. He doesn't force his knowledge on others; he always tries to get students to question and understand on their own. Harry points this out in *Deathly Hallows*, saying, "*Dumbledore usually let me find stuff out for myself. He let me try my strength, take risks.*"[7] Through these lessons, we see how teaching students to learn on their own creates a lasting impact after we are done being their teacher.

In their first lesson together Dumbledore takes Harry into a memory about the Gaunt family. Instead of simply telling Harry the information about Voldemort, he guides Harry to the discovery of Voldemort's parents:

213

> *"so Merope was…Sir, does that mean she was… Voldemort's mother?"*
>
> *"It does," said Dumbledore. "And it so happens that we also had a glimpse of Voldemort's father. I wonder whether you noticed?"*
>
> *"The Muggle Morfin attacked? The man on the horse?"*
>
> …
>
> *"And they ended up married? …*
>
> *"I think you are forgetting," said Dumbledore, "that Merope was a witch."*
>
> …
>
> *"Can you not think of any measure Merope could have taken to make Tom Riddle forget his Muggle companion, and fall in love with her instead?"*
>
> *"The Imperious Curse?" Harry suggested. "Or a love potion?"*[8]

Dumbledore already knows the importance of this memory. He has thought through every scenario. He knows that Merope Gaunt is Voldemort's mother and Tom Riddle is his father, and knows, or at least strongly believes that she used a love potion. Imagine if Dumbledore had presented the material to Harry in this manner:

> "Harry, I found something out about Voldemort that I think is very important. I would like you to make note of it and remember it forever."
>
> "Okay… what is it?" Harry says with some hesitation.
>
> "Merope Gaunt is a witch who used to live in Little Hangleton. Her brother, Morfin, attacked a Muggle named Tom Riddle who lived nearby. He was sent to Azkaban for this crime along with his father. While they were away Merope used a love potion to trick the Muggle, Tom Riddle, to marry her. They had a baby, and that baby

became the wizard we know today as Lord Voldemort. Oh, and by the way, the Gaunt family are descendants of Salazar Slytherin and speak Parseltongue."

I doubt Harry would remember much from that speech. Sure, it would sound significantly better if J.K. Rowling wrote it, but ask any student who has a teacher like Professor Binns and they'll tell you nothing is as boring as a stiff lecture. Since Dumbledore takes him into the memory and helps guide him through the importance of this moment, it ensures he still remembers them one year later when it is paramount that he understands how Voldemort thinks and acts.

Unlike Dumbledore, I am too easily frustrated when students struggle to find the answers. It's so much easier to say, 'It's the French Revolution!' or 'The answer is on page 394,' but this does little to help them in the long run. Instead, it teaches students that things will be handed to them with little to no effort. And for the most part, adults have been handing them answers all their lives. In a world where smartphones are within everyone's reach, students need to know how to find credible and reliable answers on their own. They must be able to sift through multiple news stories, perceive the bias, and develop an opinion.

During their next lessons, Dumbledore takes Harry into more memories that demonstrate Voldemort's desire to work alone, collect objects and eventually split his soul. He uses the same teaching methods each time, presents the memory, allows Harry to ask questions and helps guide him to the importance. In their last major lesson, Dumbledore gives Harry his only homework assignment: obtain Slughorn's true memory. Surprisingly, persuading Slughorn to divulge this memory is one of Harry's hardest tasks all year. Sure, instructing a student to trick their teacher into revealing their biggest regret isn't the best idea for homework. However, the thinking that went into this assignment was good practice for the real reason they're having these lessons, training Harry to go to great lengths to hunt for every last Horcrux.

After Harry successfully retrieves the memory, Dumbledore reveals that he has discovered one of the Horcruxes. He agrees to take Harry along with him to the nightmarish cave in search of Slytherin's locket. As they are walking around the lake, trying to find a way across, Harry nervously asks Dumbledore if they could just use a Summoning Charm. Rather than dismissing Harry's response, he instructs him to give it a try and as Harry yells *"Accio Horcrux"* a very large and pale figure jumps from the surface of the water causing Harry to jump backwards in surprise. Harry then asks Dumbledore if he knew this would happen and Dumbledore responds that he thought it would, but it was a good idea and *"much the simplest way of finding out what we are facing."*[9] Dismissing Harry's idea would make him feel foolish and less likely to make suggestions in the future. Instead, he allows Harry the freedom to discover for himself. Dumbledore even admits this was a much quicker way to determine what was lurking beneath the surface of the lake.

As a first year teacher, despite my many insecurities I was still confident that I was the smartest person in the room. It didn't take long to realize this was not the case. My students had a wide variety of content knowledge, but all of them had more street sense than I did. They learned skills of survival that I never had to comprehend in my own sheltered childhood. Every day my students would walk to school down streets I barely felt safe to drive on. I often witnessed robberies, police tape redirecting my route and drunks walking in the middle of the road on my commute. Once, a student was trying to persuade me to buy him some tacos from a local donut shop (no that isn't a typo, they also served Chinese food). He mistook my response of 'No' as fear, and replied, 'Don't worry, the prostitutes are only there at night time. You'll be okay.' He was eleven. These moments helped me realize that while I may be more knowledgeable about subject matter, this doesn't make me wiser than my students. In many ways they had experienced more in their eleven years than I have in an entire lifetime. Their opinions and voices needed to be heard and respected.

Professor Dumbledore's willingness to listen to the wisdom of his students makes Harry feel comfortable enough to ask any question while in his presence. Harry was raised in a household where he was forbidden to ask questions. This must be extremely difficult to deal with when sweaters are shrinking, your hair is growing unnaturally and snakes are talking to you. Since he has few other parental figures in his life, he often turns to Dumbledore for guidance. Throughout the series, Harry asks Dumbledore more questions than perhaps anyone else. In their search for the locket alone, he asks thirty-one questions from the point they leave Hogwarts until Dumbledore drinks the potion. And I'm sure he would have asked many more if the potion hadn't made Dumbledore so incoherent. Dumbledore may be intelligent and can probably multi-task, but breaking through Voldemort's defenses had to have taken some concentration. I probably would have snapped and told Harry to be quiet. But Dumbledore, as he does time and time again, welcomes all of Harry's questions.

Despite being frustrated with Dumbledore's lack of direction, in *Deathly Hallows* when Harry temporarily dies and enters his own version of Kings Cross, it is Dumbledore he pictures alongside him answering all his burning questions. A students' ability to think critically heavily relies upon their capacity to ask higher-level questions. When students do ask questions, they are more engaged with and take ownership of their learning. Just as Dumbledore does for Harry, students in our classes should feel comfortable and safe enough to ask any questions or pose any theories without fear of ridicule.

It isn't Dumbledore's knowledge that makes him wise, it is his self-insight and his understanding that a wise person never stops learning that truly makes him great. A reassuring thought as I plan for each new year. I'm still afraid I'll seem unintelligent in my students' eyes. But if Dumbledore is willing to admit he's wrong, we should be encouraged to do the same. Professor Dumbledore never lets his ideas shroud those of his students. He listens, allows others the freedom to criticize and is intelligent enough to put others' ideas before his own—the mark of a great teacher.

✳ TRUSTING ✳

Throughout the series, Harry is skeptical of Dumbledore's willingness to trust others. In particular, his trust in Professor Snape. Harry can't wrap his brain around the fact that Dumbledore trusts a man who is a former Death Eater and a frequent bully to his students. And yet Dumbledore trusts him with his life, literally, time and time again. As a young reader I was often in agreement with Harry. However, Dumbledore's willingness to trust his teachers and students turns out to be one of his greatest qualities as a headmaster.

As well as Dumbledore's overwhelming trust in Snape, we also see Dumbledore trust Hagrid and give him chance after chance in the face of criticism. In *Chamber of Secrets* Hagrid is taken away to Azkaban because of evidence that he is attempting to murder students. Can you imagine? If a teacher was accused of releasing a monster on a school full of children most principals wouldn't be so quick to back them up. Dumbledore, however, stands by him and speaks to the Minister of Magic on his behalf. When Hagrid makes mistakes during his first year of teaching and wants to quit, Dumbledore doesn't allow it and encourages him to stay on. And when McGonagall questions Dumbledore's decision to trust Hagrid while waiting for him to bring baby Harry to Privet Drive, Dumbledore simply responds that he trusts Hagrid with his life. There are countless times throughout the series when Hagrid swells with pride as he says Dumbledore has entrusted him with Hogwarts business and it only makes him want to work harder.

Other than Hagrid, Professor Dumbledore trusts Lupin and Firenze to teach at Hogwarts even though society considers them dangerous outcasts. He stands up for Trelawney when she's fired, allowing her to still call Hogwarts her home. And he sees the good in Slytherin teachers like Snape and Slughorn, even though they each have ties to the Dark Lord. Above all else, he trusts his staff. Teachers are often in a position where they have to defend themselves and an administrator's trust can have a tremendous effect.

At the same time, Professor Dumbledore puts a tremendous amount of trust in his students. When all evidence points towards Harry being the one who has opened the Chamber of Secrets, Dumbledore still believes him. When Professor Lupin was a student, Dumbledore invited him to Hogwarts knowing he was a werewolf. Even though Draco Malfoy is branded with the Dark Mark and has plotted to kill him all year, he knows Draco won't go through with it. He sees the good in all students even in the most dire of circumstances. And in many instances Dumbledore trusts Harry, Ron and Hermione to carry out tasks that he knows are above their grade level but within their capabilities. Although, I would never recommend students drop out, go on the run and hunt down a murderer, it really was a tremendous learning experience for them.

Throughout the series we get the feeling that Harry trusts Dumbledore with almost anything. He feels comfortable enough to tell him any theory, ask any question and discuss any topic. However, there was one time in the series when Harry absolutely did not want to seek out Dumbledore for help. In *Order of the Phoenix* Dumbledore has distanced himself from Harry because he believes it would help protect him, but this distance only makes Harry feel like he was a nuisance. This is a great reminder that a teacher's work is never done. Students are watching us at every moment. A deliberate connection can make all the difference but one negative comment can destroy a relationship.

Professor Dumbledore places his trust in people who don't always deserve it and this earns him the greatest respect. J.K. Rowling writes: *"He was often described as the greatest wizard of the age, but that wasn't why Harry respected him. You couldn't help trusting Albus Dumbledore.*"[10] It is this trust that makes those around him want to achieve more. Imagine what our students can accomplish if we put the same amount of trust in them as Dumbledore puts in others.

✳ ✳ ✳

Even though he's widely considered the most intelligent wizard, this doesn't stop Dumbledore from relating with his students. He comically conducts the Weasley twins off-key version of the Hogwarts song, pretends to be temporarily deaf when Harry calls Rita Skeeter a cow and even wears a silly hat from a Christmas popper to dinner. These moments, along with his enthusiastic love of candy, help students realize that their headmaster isn't just brilliant, he's also funny, which helps them relax in his presence.

As a young girl reading the series, it was easy for me to picture Dumbledore as perfect. Children often view their own teachers as flawless, and to me, Dumbledore was the ideal mentor. Upon rereading the series it became evident that Dumbledore didn't always have Harry's best interest in mind. As we reach the final book, we realize that even the great Dumbledore has regrets. Harry struggles through these revelations of Dumbledore's imperfections alongside us, finally coming to the conclusion that it doesn't matter what happened in Dumbledore's past. To Harry and myself, he will always be an inspiration to do what is right and just. Our past errors should not prevent us from moving forward and making the most of the life we have ahead.

Dumbledore, like everyone, has flaws, but he is still an extraordinary teacher and headmaster. As Elphias Doge writes in his obituary:

> *"Albus Dumbledore was never proud or vain; he could find something to value in anyone, however apparently insignificant or wretched, and I believe that his early losses endowed him with greater humanity and sympathy... That*

he was the most inspiring and the best loved of all Hogwarts headmasters cannot be in question."[11]

Professor Dumbledore works tirelessly to protect and educate all students at Hogwarts. No matter if they are an orphaned boy, an outcast werewolf or a snobby pureblood, he shows them compassion and believes in them one hundred percent. Dumbledore teaches us that this profession is as rewarding as the work we put into it: *"There is nothing more important than passing on ancient skills, helping hone young minds."[12]* He even confessed once that *"His greatest pleasure lay in teaching."[13]* I couldn't agree more.

EPILOGUE

Nineteen Professors Later

"We teachers are rather good at magic, you know."[1]

On my best days, my teaching style most closely aligns with Professor Lupin's. Like him, my personality is more reserved, I try to choose the morally right paths and I view myself as an outcast. Inside our classrooms, however, we both try our best to develop relationships with our students and engage them with our subject matter. Through the process of writing this book, I have come to realize that I have characteristics of all nineteen professors, not just the exemplary ones like Lupin. At the beginning of the year I'm as strict as McGonagall, but I often lose heart towards the end like Hagrid. I try to be accepting of all students like Sprout, but still end up with favorites like Slughorn. And it really depends on how much caffeine I have consumed to determine if I'll welcome questions like Dumbledore or shut them down like Umbridge. The Hogwarts professors represent a wide variety of teaching styles, and as my experiences have indicated, I will never perfectly align with just one professor.

One of the big themes of the Harry Potter series is that people are not easily categorized. Arguably, no one fits inside the rigid characteristics of any one Hogwarts house. I want to belong in Gryffindor, but I am reminded that I'm also loyal, intelligent and ambitious so I could easily be a member of the other three. Harry was almost placed in Slytherin and Hermione is clearly intelligent enough to belong in Ravenclaw. Hufflepuff's Cedric Diggory had more bravery than Gryffindor's Peter Pettigrew, and even though he's a main antagonist and the pride of Slytherin, Draco Malfoy would have never killed Dumbledore.

Just as one person doesn't fit perfectly within the house system, great teachers don't have to be the most intelligent, charismatic or strict. A Ravenclaw doesn't automatically make a better professor than a Hufflepuff, Gryffindor or Slytherin. Even when handed identical lesson plans, every teacher and every classroom looks different.

The Hogwarts professors show us that even the most unlikely of characters have the ability to transform their students' lives. It's a Death Eater that persuades Harry to become an Auror, a werewolf that teaches him to defend himself from monsters and a witch who can transfigure herself into a cat that shows him the true meaning of bravery. Wizard, witch, ghost, werewolf, centaur, part-goblin, half-giant, or even Death Eater—we learn from them that there isn't just one correct teaching style. While the Hogwarts professors teach magic, Muggle teachers, like myself, need to remember "We do not need magic to change the world, we carry all the power we need inside ourselves already."[2] No matter our background, our personality or our abilities, everyone can become a magical teacher.

ACKNOWLEDGEMENTS

HOUSE POINTS

I would like to thank the people who made this book possible.

First, thanks to my amazing Ravenclaw brother, Jason, who is the smartest person I know. You believed in this book before anyone else. Thank you for spending countless hours discussing the Hogwarts professors with me. And more importantly, thank you for editing every single section of this book. Without you this book would not be possible. Or at least, it would not be as good. I will always cherish those long hours we spent in my makeshift office surrounded by crumpled up papers and Harry Potter posters hung with blue painter's tape for inspiration. I will never be able to repay you for helping this dream become a reality.

To my Mom, who gave me a love for reading. You made weekly trips to the library seem like an adventure as we cut through the dirt path and bushes of the 'jungle' on our way to the door. You always let us pick out as many books as we wanted, sometimes leaving with a stack that was as tall as Dobby's collection of knit hats. Because of you, I still consider the library a magical place. And when people told you the Harry Potter books were not good for kids, you read them yourself and immediately handed *Sorcerer's Stone* to me with contagious enthusiasm. Without you, I would not have Harry's world as an escape. Thank you, also, for teaching me that learning can be fun. As one of my first teachers, you showed me that school wasn't a chore. It was a chance to explore, discover and grow. Your passion would rival Flitwick's and I hope to emulate this in my classroom each day.

To my Dad, who made me believe anything is possible. When you wanted a new door that would give quicker access to the pool, I watched you take a sledgehammer to the wall in the middle of winter—even allowing me a few swings. That breezy hole was a reminder that the outcome is worth the effort. And later, I watched you walk away from a stable career to pursue your dream of owning your own company. When it came time to choose which school I wanted to work at, your actions showed me that sometimes we have to be brave and follow our hearts. And when I told you I wanted to write a teaching book on Harry Potter, without yet having read a single word, you immediately opened your computer to find a way to contact J.K. Rowling to tell her all about it.

To my brother, Chris, and my sister-in-law, Danielle (name thief!), who are always fully on board with my Harry Potter shenanigans. When I told you I wanted to fly to London to see the Cursed Child and some locations in the film, you simply asked "When do we leave?" And even years after Harry's scar stopped hurting, every time I bring up a new theory around the dinner table, you enthusiastically join in.

To my friend, Tori, who helps make me be a better teacher. Without your friendship and guidance, I would have more days like Trelawney or Hagrid and less like Lupin. You make work incredibly fun and you challenge me to be better for my students. And thanks for letting me write about you in this book. I'm sorry I included stories of you telling me to get my shit together instead of times where we laughed so hard we couldn't stop. But only you and I find it funny when you sing Jingle Bells while popping bubble wrap to match the tune. You have made a bigger impact on my life than you realize and you are an amazing friend—even though you refer to Ron Weasley as Kevin.

To my friend, Selena, who helped encourage my Harry Potter obsession. Thank you for your unfailing belief in this book. Your enthusiasm helped give me the confidence needed to put these words out there for others.

I would also like to thank my uncle, Chris Howard, for his amazing cover art and for his support of this book. Check out his art and writings at saltwaterwitch.com.

And finally, to J.K. Rowling, thank you for your stories. They have made me a better person and teacher. And I apologize now if my Dad tries to contact you.

NOTES

INTRODUCTION

[1]J.K. Rowling, *Harry Potter and the Sorcerer's Stone* (New York: Scholastic Press, 1998), pp. 252-253.

PROFESSOR SPROUT

[1] J.K. Rowling, *Harry Potter and the Half-Blood Prince* (New York: Scholastic Press, 2005), p. 627.
[2] J.K. Rowling, *Harry Potter and the Goblet of Fire* (New York: Scholastic Press, 2000), p. 176-177.
[3] J.K. Rowling, *Harry Potter and the Order of the Phoenix* (New York: Scholastic Press, 2003), pp. 204-205.
[4] Jessica Roy, "Behind Creepypasta, the Internet Community That Allegedly Spread a Killer Meme," *Time*, March 30, 2020.
[5] Susan Cain, *Quiet* (New York: Broadway Books, 2012).
[6] *Half-Blood Prince*, p. 627.

PROFESSOR FLITWICK

[1] *Sorcerer's Stone*, p. 171.
[2] *Order of the Phoenix*, p. 311.
[3] *Sorcerer's Stone*, p. 171.
[4] *Half-Blood Prince*, p. 515.
[5] *Sorcerer's Stone*, p. 171.
[6] Robert L. Fried, *The Passionate Teacher* (Boston: Beacon Press, 2001), p. 19.
[7] *The Passionate Teacher*, p. 23.

PROFESSOR MCGONAGALL

[1] *Sorcerer's Stone*, p. 134.
[2] *Sorcerer's Stone*, p. 113.
[3] *Half-Blood Prince*, p. 88.
[4] *Order of the Phoenix*, 320-321.
[5] J.K. Rowling, *Harry Potter and the Chamber of Secrets* (New York: Scholastic Press, 1999), p. 284.
[6] *Order of the Phoenix*, p. 257.
[7] *Sorcerer's Stone*, pp. 145, 134.
[8] *Sorcerer's Stone*, p. 269.
[9] J.K. Rowling, *Harry Potter and the Prisoner of Azkaban (*New York: Scholastic Press, 1999*)*, p. 150.
[10] *Order of the Phoenix*, p. 320.
[11] *Chamber of Secrets*, p. 144.
[12] *Order of the Phoenix*, pp. 247-248.
[13] *Sorcerer's Stone*, p. 134.
[14] *Half-Blood Prince*, p. 174.
[15] *Order of the Phoenix*, p. 665.
[16] *Prisoner of Azkaban*, p. 109.
[17] *Chamber of Secrets*, p. 264.
[18] *Order of the Phoenix*, p. 730.

PROFESSOR SNAPE

[1] *Order of the Phoenix*, p. 232.
[2] *Chamber of Secrets*, p. 77.
[3] *Sorcerer's Stone*, pp. 136-137.
[4] *Prisoner of Azkaban*, p. 123.
[5] *Sorcerer's Stone*, p. 300.

[6] *Sorcerer's Stone*, pp. 126, 137.
[7] *Half-Blood Prince*, pp. 177-178.
[8] *Sorcerer's Stone*, p. 137.
[9] *Order of the Phoenix*, pp. 232-233.
[10] *Order of the Phoenix*, pp. 233-234.
[11] *Sorcerer's Stone*, pp. 137, 136.
[12] *Half-Blood Prince*, p. 460.
[13] *Order of the Phoenix*, p. 746.
[14] *Prisoner of Azkaban*, pp. 360, 172.
[15] *Sorcerer's Stone*, p. 139.
[16] *Prisoner of Azkaban*, pp. 125-126, 132.

PROFESSOR SLUGHORN

[1] *Half-Blood Prince*, p. 474.
[2] *Half-Blood Prince*, pp. 186, 187.
[3] *Half-Blood Prince*, pp. 187-188.
[4] *Sorcerer's Stone*, p. 285.
[5] *Half-Blood Prince*, p. 188.
[6] *Half-Blood Prince*, p. 378.
[7] *Half-Blood Prince*, pp. 75-76.
[8] *Half-Blood Prince*, pp. 70, 86.

HAGRID

[1] *Prisoner of Azkaban*, pp. 112-113.
[2] *Sorcerer's Stone*, p. 49.
[3] *Prisoner of Azkaban*, p. 112.
[4] *Prisoner of Azkaban*, pp. 114, 118.
[5] *Prisoner of Azkaban*, p. 293.
[6] *Prisoner of Azkaban*, p. 220.
[7] *Prisoner of Azkaban*, p. 317.
[8] Stephen Covey, *The 7 Habits of Highly Effective People: Powerful Lessons in Personal Change* (New York: Simon & Schuster, 2013), p. 299.

PROFESSOR GRUBBLY-PLANK

[1] *Order of the Phoenix*, p. 258.
[2] *Order of the Phoenix*, p. 261.
[3] *Goblet of Fire*, p. 497.
[4] *Order of the Phoenix*, p. 259.
[5] *Goblet of Fire*, p. 436.

PROFESSOR TRELAWNEY

[1] *Prisoner of Azkaban*, p. 102.
[2] *Prisoner of Azkaban*, p. 102.
[3] *Prisoner of Azkaban*, pp. 103-104, 107.
[4] *Prisoner of Azkaban*, pp. 228, 229.
[5] *Order of the Phoenix*, p. 314.
[6] *Prisoner of Azkaban*, p. 298.

FIRENZE

[1] *Sorcerer's Stone*, p. 257.
[2] *Order of the Phoenix*, pp. 600-601.
[3] *Order of the Phoenix*, pp. 603-604.

MADAM HOOCH

[1] *Sorcerer's Stone*, p. 146.
[2] *Sorcerer's Stone*, p. 146.

[3] *Sorcerer's Stone*, p. 146.
[4] *Sorcerer's Stone*, pp. 146-147.

PROFESSOR SINISTRA

[1] *Order of the Phoenix*, p. 224.

PROFESSOR BINNS

[1] *Chamber of Secrets*, p. 149.
[2] *Sorcerer's Stone*, p. 133.
[3] *Chamber of Secrets*, p. 148.
[4] *Sorcerer's Stone*, p. 133.
[5] *Order of the Phoenix*, pp. 355, 228.
[6] *Chamber of Secrets*, p. 148.
[7] *Order of the Phoenix*, p. 356.
[8] *Sorcerer's Stone*, p. 263.

PROFESSOR QUIRRELL

[1] *Sorcerer's Stone*, p. 70.
[2] *Sorcerer's Stone*, p. 85.
[3] *Sorcerer's Stone*, p. 70.
[4] *Sorcerer's Stone*, p. 134.
[5] *Sorcerer's Stone*, p. 172.
[6] *Half-Blood Prince*, p. 512.
[7] *Order of the Phoenix*, p. 317.
[8] *Sorcerer's Stone*, p. 71.

PROFESSOR LOCKHART

[1] *Chamber of Secrets*, p. 100.
[2] *Chamber of Secrets*, p. 60.
[3] *Chamber of Secrets*, pp. 161-162.
[4] *Chamber of Secrets*, pp. 101, 102.
[5] *Chamber of Secrets*, pp. 190, 191, 192-193.
[6] *Chamber of Secrets*, pp, 251, 331.

PROFESSOR LUPIN

[1] *Prisoner of Azkaban*, p. 155.
[2] *Prisoner of Azkaban*, pp. 132, 133.
[3] *Prisoner of Azkaban*, p. 134.
[4] *Prisoner of Azkaban*, p. 135.
[5] *Prisoner of Azkaban*, p. 289.
[6] *Prisoner of Azkaban*, p. 156.
[7] *Prisoner of Azkaban*, p. 187.
[8] *Prisoner of Azkaban*, p. 239.
[9] *Prisoner of Azkaban*, p. 246.
[10] *Prisoner of Azkaban*, pp. 90, 86.
[11] J.K. Rowling, *Harry Potter and the Deathly Hallows* (New York: Scholastic Press, 2007), p. 204.
[12] *Prisoner of Azkaban*, p. 424.

PROFESSOR MOODY

[1] *Goblet of Fire*, p. 217.
[2] *Goblet of Fire*, pp. 211-212.
[3] *Goblet of Fire*, p. 213.
[4] *Goblet of Fire*, pp. 216, 217.
[5] *Goblet of Fire*, p. 232.
[6] *Goblet of Fire*, p. 208.
[7] *Goblet of Fire*, p. 204.

[8] *Goblet of Fire*, p. 206.
[9] *Goblet of Fire*, pp. 218, 219, 220.
[10] *Goblet of Fire*, p. 344.
[11] *Goblet of Fire*, p. 477.
[12] *Goblet of Fire*, p. 243.

PROFESSOR UMBRIDGE

[1] *Order of the Phoenix*, p. 239.
[2] *Order of the Phoenix*, p. 203.
[3] *Order of the Phoenix*, pp. 212, 213.
[4] *Order of the Phoenix*, p. 240.
[5] *Order of the Phoenix*, p. 242.
[6] *Order of the Phoenix*, p. 243.
[7] Ken Robinson, *Creative Schools* (New York: Penguin Books), p. xx.
[8] *Order of the Phoenix*, pp. 244, 245, 246.
[9] *Order of the Phoenix*, p. 317.
[10] *Order of the Phoenix*, p. 245.
[11] *Goblet of Fire*, pp. 721, 722.
[12] *Goblet of Fire*, p. 724.

HARRY POTTER

[1] *Order of the Phoenix*, p. 394.
[2] *Sorcerer's Stone*, p. 297.
[3] *Order of the Phoenix*, p. 392.
[4] Andrea Culver, "Writing to Learn," Teaching Channel. https://learn.teachingchannel.com/video/writing-to-learn.
[5] *Order of the Phoenix*, p. 344.
[6] *Order of the Phoenix*, p. 394.
[7] *Order of the Phoenix*, p. 397.
[8] *Order of the Phoenix*, p. 606.

PROFESSOR DUMBLEDORE

[1] *Chamber of Secrets*, p. 264.
[2] *Sorcerer's Stone*, p. 123.
[3] *Sorcerer's Stone*, p. 297.
[4] *Goblet of Fire*, p. 680.
[5] *Chamber of Secrets*, p. 333.
[6] *Sorcerer's Stone*, pp. 214, 298.
[7] *Deathly Hallows*, p. 433.
[8] *Half-Blood Prince*, pp. 213-214.
[9] *Half-Blood Prince*, pp. 561-562.
[10] *Prisoner of Azkaban*, p. 91.
[11] *Deathly Hallow*, p. 20.
[12] *Half-Blood Prince*, p. 442.
[13] *Deathly Hallow*, p. 16.

EPILOGUE

[1] *Deathly Hallows*, p. 595.
[2] J.K. Rowling, *Very Good Lives: The Fringe Benefits of Failure, and the Importance of Imagination* (New York: Little, Brown and Company, 2008).

ABOUT THE AUTHOR

Danielle Dickie is a Muggle teacher who has worked with intermediate and secondary students in California's Central Valley. She was once recognized as Educator of the Week by local news—even though other days were more magical. She has a bachelor's in social science with a secondary teaching emphasis and a master's in teaching. Her house is filled with 126 Harry Potter books in 7 different languages. She supports Liverpool F.C. and is in Gryffindor. But her dog, Lily, shows most of the bravery.

Made in the USA
Columbia, SC
11 July 2021